The nature and pattern of family–friendly employment policies in Britain

Shirley Dex and Colin Smith

The POLICY
PP
PRESS

First published in Great Britain in April 2002 by

The Policy Press
34 Tyndall's Park Road
Bristol BS8 1PY
UK

Tel no +44 (0)117 954 6800
Fax no +44 (0)117 973 7308
E-mail tpp@bristol.ac.uk
www.policypress.org.uk

Published for the Joseph Rowntree Foundation by The Policy Press

ISBN 1 86134 433 3

Shirley Dex is currently a Principal Research Fellow at the Judge Institute of Management, University of Cambridge, and **Colin Smith** was formerly a Research Fellow in the ESRC Centre for Business Research and the Geography Department, University of Cambridge and currently works in the Government Economic Service.

The **Joseph Rowntree Foundation** has supported this project as part of its programme of research and innovative development projects, which it hopes will be of value to policy makers, practitioners and service users. The facts presented and views expressed in this report are, however, those of the authors and not necessarily those of the Foundation.

Front cover: image supplied by EyeWire
Cover design by Qube Design Associates, Bristol
Printed in Great Britain by Hobbs the Printers Ltd, Southampton

Contents

List of tables, figures and boxes

Tables

Figures

Boxes

Acknowledgements

We wish to thank the Data Archive at the
University of Essex for supplying the Workplace
Employee Relations Survey (WERS) data and the
funders of the data, for giving us permission to
use the data for the analyses contained in this
report; namely the Department of Trade and
Industry, the Economic and Social Research
Council, and the Advisory, Conciliation and
Arbitration Service. The data on the 1998 FTSE100
companies were collected by Rathbone
Investment Management. Dr Sally Winter
organised the data collection. We are grateful to
Rathbone Investment Management for permission
to carry out further analyses on these data, which
were transmitted to us in an anonymised form.
We also thank participants of the Family Policy
Studies Centre seminar for useful suggestions as
well as some individuals who have given more
detailed comments on an earlier draft: Mark
Beatson, Frank Wilkinson, Peter Nolan, Ceridwen
Roberts and Barbara Ballard. We are, of course,
responsible for these analyses and any
interpretations attached to them.

Introduction

There has been growing interest in family-friendly working arrangements, often referred to as work–life balance policies. In the context of growing business and family pressures, this interest in more flexible working arrangements has developed as a potential way of helping families and employers to cope with the real life problems of being carers and employees in a competitive business environment. There have been growing pressures on companies and workplaces to become more efficient and more competitive in the global economy. Alongside these have gone growing family pressures from marital breakdown, increasing income inequalities, pressures on families to have two incomes and growing caring responsibilities. Both of these sets of developments are well charted in earlier reviews (Dex, 1999). It is undoubtedly the case that societies face a challenge if they are to balance paid work and caring needs (Daly, 1996). It is therefore perhaps not surprising that government initiatives have emerged to address some of these issues.

Action to enable men and women to reconcile the demands of work with the demands of their home life has received prominence following European Union (EU) directives and new policy and legislative intentions of the 1997 Labour government to implement the various directives. Policy makers have hoped that family-friendly working arrangements might have a contribution to make. The policy and legislative agendas have been moving at a fast pace in Britain since 1997, and somewhat ahead of the research and evidence base relating to flexible working arrangements as set out in Box 1.

While the statistical picture of the extent of such flexible working arrangements is now fairly well charted, although with a few gaps, there are many questions left unanswered. There is still a need for a more detailed understanding of which employers offer such arrangements to their employees, but also of which employees are entitled to access these provisions. We are not so clear about the main drivers that motivated organisations to adopt the family-friendly policies they have chosen. A better understanding of their motivation and any predisposing or encouraging factors that led them to adopt such working arrangements would help initiatives aiming to encourage a wider range of employers to do the same. The extent to which there are positive or negative outcomes from having flexible working arrangements is also under-researched. While we have some limited case study evidence on the outcomes, an overview from a large-scale and representative set of employers is needed. We also need a greater understanding of whether business outcomes and performance are influenced by family-friendly policies after controlling for some of the other well-known influences on performance. It may be that good performance outcomes found in case studies result from something other than family-friendly policies, or are limited to the case study companies because they have other features that predisposed them to success.

All of these questions required large-scale survey data containing a range of information about each organisation. Such data would allow for multivariate analyses to be carried out, which would help to disentangle the effects of family-friendly policies from other potential explanations of the outcomes. Up to the mid-1990s, there were no large-scale representative employer surveys in Britain that included questions on family-friendly working arrangements alongside a range of other data about the employer. But this has now changed.

Box 1: Summary of the policy and legislative developments since 1997 relevant to development of flexible working arrangements

Working Time Directive (1998)
A European directive laying down a maximum of 48 hours (averaged over 17, 26 or even 52 weeks) came into force in October 1998. This directive also confers a right to three weeks paid annual leave, rising to four in November 1999, and minimum weekly rest periods.

The Part-time Work Directive (2000)
This was agreed in December 1997 to come into force by July 2000 to ensure that part-time workers receive no less favourable treatment than full-time workers in terms of pay, holidays, public holidays, access to occupational pension schemes, sick pay, maternity/parental leave and training.

National Child Care Strategy (1998)
A framework and consultation on childcare provision in Britain (DfEE, 1998).

National Strategy for Carers (1999)
A framework and consultation on provisions for the needs of those caring for older people in Britain (DoH, 1999).

Parental Leave Directive (from 15 December 1999)
The 1999 Employment Relations Act gave working parents the right to take unpaid leave of 13 weeks for each child born after 15 December 1999 up to the child's fifth birthday implementing the Parental Leave Directive. An extension to these arrangements was announced on 25 April 2001 in a Department of Trade and Industry Press Release extending the time off from 13 to 18 weeks for parents of disabled children, and the basic arrangements were to be extended to all children who were under the age of five at 15 December 1999.

Time off for dependants (1999)
The 1999 Employment Relations Act gave working parents the right to take a reasonable amount of time off work to deal with uncertain, unexpected or sudden emergencies involving people who depend on them, and to make any necessary longer-term arrangements.

Work–life balance: Changing patterns in a changing world (2000)
This launched an initiative to widen the extent of flexible working arrangements in Britain (DfEE, 2000), including the Work–life Balance Challenge Fund offering help to employers to introduce flexible working arrangements.

The Work and Parents Taskforce (2001)
Set up by the Department of Trade and Industry to consider the possibility of new light-touch legislation giving employees a right to request flexible working arrangements.

Work and parents: Competitiveness and choice
A Green Paper (DTI, 2000b).

The 2001 Budget announced forthcoming changes to:
* extension of *maternity leave*, from 18 to 26 weeks from April 2003;
* increases in *maternity pay*, paid adoption leave from 2003;
* right to two weeks paid *paternity leave* from 2003.

This report presents the findings from a newly available 1997/98 dataset, the British Workplace Employee Relations Survey (WERS) (Airy et al, 1999), that provided valuable information about which British employers had family-friendly working arrangements in 1998 alongside a wide range of other information about the employers' characteristics, employee relations, human resources (HR) policies, workforce profile and performance. This survey has been carried out at regular intervals in Britain since 1980, but only in 1998 did it include questions on employers' family-friendly policies and employees' access to them. In fact, the 1998 survey struck out in a large number of new and innovative directions which offer more potential for explanation than any of its earlier versions. These high quality data, with a very high response rate for an employer survey, therefore provided a uniquely valuable opportunity to add knowledge to the debates that have been taking place in Britain about flexible working arrangements. They enabled a consideration to be made of whether there were systematic reasons associated with offering employees certain types of working arrangements, and whether family-friendly policies are associated with certain outcomes for employees and for business performance.

Background

Family-friendly working was initially a corporate-led development in the UK, the US and Australia motivated by national concern about the shrinking pool of labour caused by the declining fertility rate (Berry-Lound, 1990; Spearritt and Edgar, 1994), and in response to having women employees facing issues of family formation (Forth et al, 1997). While this first motivation was linked to women, there has been a recognition that men as fathers and other workers also have interests in, and can benefit from, flexible working arrangements, for a variety of personal and caring reasons. Research in Britain also identified the proactive role played by unions in the development of family-friendly working arrangements, especially in the public sector in Britain (Forth et al, 1997).

Over the period in which family-friendly policies started to emerge in British companies, there were major elements of deregulation in the labour market. During the 1980s, the regulative framework for the labour market in Britain underwent a series of changes described as promoting labour market flexibility. The government's rationale for the package of new measures was described as supporting economic growth by promoting a competitive, efficient and flexible labour market. This aim was seen as a vital element if Britain was to survive in the increasingly competitive product markets of Europe and the rest of the world.

Probably the main change in the framework came from the decline in trades union coverage and the associated increasing fragmentation of the system of pay determination in Britain in the 1980s. Unions were blamed for the lack of organisation restructuring and for Britain's poor productivity and economic performance. It is against a background of declining trades unions that flexible working arrangements grew. Some commentators have suggested that the two trends are not unrelated (for example Casey et al, 1997), and that the decline of trades unions allowed employers to introduce certain types of flexible working that previously would not have been possible. However, Forth et al's earlier work pointed to the opposite conclusion, suggesting that unions were linked to the new developments in family-friendly working arrangements. The research contained in this report allows us to take a further look at the relationships between unions and certain types of flexible employment.

Concepts of family–friendly working

When a decision was made to introduce new questions into the Workplace Employee Relations Survey, the term **family-friendly policies** was still in vogue, and this was how the new module of questions was described. By the time the data were released, the term and concept that lay behind it had been largely replaced by a new term: **work–life balance**. Work–life balance has a much wider focus on all employees and their personal lives outside of work. We have retained the term 'family-friendly' for use in this report for a number of reasons: partly because it was our original title, and also because our project is part of a programme of research on work and family life. However, the data we analyse are not restricted to workers with children: they cut across the whole spectrum of workers.

The wide range of policies that have been assumed under the heading of 'family friendly' or 'work–life balance' precludes a concise definition. There are policies concerned with employees' hours of work (job sharing, part-time work, flexitime), leave entitlements (parental leave, career break), location of work (workplace or home) financial assistance (childcare, maternity pay) and particular responsibilities, for example elder care or children. Clearly, there is a need to consider formal policies as well as more informal working arrangements, although the latter may well have been neglected in survey questions (Dex and Scheibl, 2001).

There is also in the literature a recognition that not all flexible working arrangements will be genuinely friendly to families. For one thing, the practices of companies are not always the same as their policies might suggest. In addition, employers' provisions of flexible working arrangements have been for a variety of motives, with some being wholly for the benefit of the employer (for example Casey et al, 1997; Purcell, 1997; Purcell et al, 1999). This report does not consider other so-called flexible types of work, such as temporary contracts or self-employment. Other Joseph Rowntree Foundation projects are considering, more directly, the issues of what is genuinely family-friendly to employees (for example Bond et al, 2002; Dex and Scheibl, 2002). In this report we focus only on the incidence of certain flexible working arrangements covered in our data.

The extent of family-friendly working policies and practices up to 1998

The extent of family-friendly policies and practices can be measured through the extent of employees who benefit, and through the proportion of employers who offer them, respectively. A cautious interpretation of the available information on employers' provisions in the early 1990s suggested that family-friendly policies and practices were not widespread among British employers and were most prevalent in the public sector and larger companies (Brannen et al, 1994).

This view was supported by the findings of two large-scale studies by the Policy Studies Institute (PSI) (McRae, 1991; Forth et al, 1997). Taking different types of policy separately, 9 out of 10 employers in 1996 provided at least one family-friendly arrangement; two thirds provided two or more. These proportions were boosted considerably by including maternity and paternity-related provisions (Forth et al, 1997). The most common provision was flexible or non-standard working hours, with 71% of employers having such arrangements. The same PSI study reported that firms voluntarily providing all four categories of family-friendly initiatives, defined as 'model employers' (in excess of statutory maternity benefits, paternity leave, childcare arrangements and non-standard working hours) were found to constitute just 5% of employers. The 'model employer' had a very clear profile, being large and unionised. While the private sector made a lower level of provision than the public sector, there was a slightly better level of provision when the private company was unionised and large (Forth et al, 1997, pp 152-5).

Key questions for this research

Our research set out to investigate the following key questions:

- Which employers have family-friendly policies and practices, and what has encouraged them to adopt such policies?
- How many employees take up the provisions?
- Which groups of employees are eligible to benefit from family-friendly provisions? Are employers cherry-picking, offering fringe benefits to their most valued employees?
- Do employees know about their employers' policies?
- Do family-friendly policies make a difference to employees?
- Are family-friendly working arrangements value for money? What are the costs and benefits? What are the effects on business performance?

The data sources

Our main data source for addressing these questions was the Workplace Employee Relations Survey (WERS), as described in more detail below.

The Workplace Employee Relations Survey 1998[1]

The WERS data were collected from October 1997 to June 1998 and involved interviews with managers and workers in over 2,191 workplaces and questionnaires from 28,323 employees from these same workplaces. The response rate obtained for the manager survey was 80%. The survey also contained a panel element link to the earlier 1990 WIRS survey, but this is not used in the analyses described in this report. The 1998 survey had a new sampling base: establishments with a minimum of 10 employees. The earlier surveys had taken a minimum of 25 employees. This means that the survey as a whole represents 15.8 million employees, or approximately three quarters of all employees in employment in Britain in 1998. Incorporating employees into the survey was also a new innovation. The technical details of the survey are described in Airy et al (1999).

There were also new additions to the content of the 1998 survey. Along with its past coverage of the nature of collective representation and bargaining, it included new questions on equal opportunities policies, family-friendly policies, performance indicators, payment systems and performance appraisal, recruitment and training, quality improvement schemes and the individualisation of employment contracts. These new questions, in combination with others in the WERS, provided a valuable opportunity to examine the nature and patterns of family-friendly policies in Britain in the late 1990s using the main cross-sectional survey.

Family-friendly working arrangements in the WERS

The manager questionnaire asked about the working arrangements that the firm offered as entitlements to non-managerial employees. The provisions covered:

- parental leave
- job sharing
- term-time working only
- working at or from home during normal working hours
- ability to change from full- to part-time hours
- workplace or other nursery provision
- help with the costs of childcare
- flexi-time.

The wording of the WERS questions is not specifically about organisation policies. In this sense we might expect that answers covered both formal policies and practices of the establishments in the survey, albeit only for non-managerial employees. However, the fact that the question wording used 'entitlement' implies that informal arrangements, especially if subject to a manager's discretion, would be less likely to be counted.

In addition, another two provisions were asked about but not in a way that was restricted to non-managerial employees:

- paternity leave; and
- scheme for time off for emergencies.

Although this is a list of 10 arrangements, there is a risk of double counting in the case of parental leave and paternity leave. At the time of this survey, 'parental leave' was not well defined since there were no statutory arrangements in Britain and the term is easily confused with maternity or paternity leave, perhaps more so by employees than employers. This should be borne in mind in examining these data. These two arrangements were collapsed into one (either/or) arrangement for some analyses, particularly for counting the number of policies.

Employees' questions in the WERS

In addition, employees were asked whether their employer made family-friendly provision available to them, using six of the same provisions used in questions to employers. In principle, this makes it possible to match up the employees' responses with those of their employers to see if they are consistent. The family-friendly arrangements used in questions to employees consisted of:

- parental leave
- job sharing

---

[1] The fourth WERS, in 1998, was sponsored by the Department of Trade and Industry, the Economic and Social Research Council, the (former) Employment Department, the PSI and the Advisory, Conciliation and Arbitration Service, and was collected by Social Community and Planning Research (SCPR), now renamed the National Centre for Social Research (NCSR).

- working at or from home during normal working hours
- workplace or other nursery provision or help with childcare
- scheme for time off for emergencies
- flexi-time.

A comparison of employers' and employees' sources of data on the same policies shows that there is a large measure of inconsistency in the replies about whether employees thought they had or did not have entitlement to the relevant policies. The employee question wording left room for ambiguity in the employees' interpretations of the questions asked. Individuals could have thought arrangements were not available to them because they did not think they needed them. However, errors can occur in all survey responses. If we assume that all managers' responses were reasonably correct, the employee data may point to organisations either offering family-friendly working arrangements to selected non-managerial employees only, or failing to communicate with all employees about the provisions they offer. A further analysis of employee awareness is contained in Dex et al (2002).

Other WERS data

Part of the value of the WERS was that it contained a wide range of other information from employers and employees that can be used to explain some of the phenomena we are interested in. Full lists of the variables considered in our analysis are provided in the four technical papers linked to this report (Dex and Smith, 2001a, b, c; Dex et al, 2001). One of our initial tasks was to check for correlations between these potential explanatory variables, and to recode or eliminate as necessary, since the analysis assumes they are independent of each other.

Other sources

Two other sources of data were available to us. One was the (former) DfEE/PSI Employers' Survey of Firms' Family-Friendly Working Arrangements from 1996. This had information on a range of family-friendly employer provisions, but only a narrow range of other employer characteristics. Although we analysed this survey, we are unable to report any of the findings in this

report, partly through space constraints. Where the earlier data overlapped with the WERS data, we did not find any conflicting findings.

The other dataset consisted of information on family-friendly policies from a telephone and postal survey of the Financial Times Stock Exchange largest 100 companies in 1998 (FTSE100) merged with data from their published company reports. This dataset was used to investigate the link between family-friendly policies and performance and the main conclusions are reported in the Appendix.

What can the WERS data contribute?

Since the WERS data were unusually high quality for an employer survey of this kind, the WERS offers a representative picture of the sort that one hopes for from large-scale survey data. The wide range of contextual data in the WERS provides a very rich source of explanatory variables for use in the analyses.

The intention in all cases was to carry out multivariate analyses. **Multivariate analysis** constitutes a set of statistical techniques in which one variable is the focus to be explained, the dependent variable, and other measures are used as potential explanations of variations in the dependent variable. These statistical techniques allow for a pseudo-laboratory experiment to take place, to find the effect of one (unit of) input, when other potential influences are controlled, in this case by statistics rather than by laboratory conditions. These procedures permit the separate effects of different influences to be identified and disentangled and their relative importance to be determined. So, in the example of organisations having adopted family-friendly policies, we are able to identify the factors associated with that adoption, and their relative importance.

The WERS data we used were cross-sectional in nature, all relevant to the time they were collected. This means that our analysis could find only statistically significant associations. It could not uncover causal relations: for that, longitudinal data would be needed, which would follow the same companies over time and could relate their current outcomes to earlier behaviour.

Survey questions of the kind contained in the WERS data are not intended to give an in-depth insight into respondents' feelings or meanings. Survey data have to be succinct and sometimes simplifying. What we do not get from the analyses of survey data is the rich detail and discursive accounts of employer practices and workplace cultures in which the survey measures are located and played out. Such qualitative data are important in filling in the whole picture, and qualitative data on these topics have resulted from some of the other studies in the Joseph Rowntree Foundation Work and Family Life Programme, of which this statistical analysis is one part. However, the WERS data are important especially in understanding the extent to which relationships that have been found in other smaller-scale studies are representative and statistically significant.

Plan of the report

This report is a summary of more extensive considerations of the questions we set out to answer. In order to make the report accessible, we have included the full technical details and results in a series of technical papers (Dex and Smith, 2001a, b, c; Dex et al, 2001), which can be obtained by interested readers in pdf format.

Chapters 2 and 3 constitute a section in which we consider which companies and employees have family-friendly policies. Chapter 2 examines the adoption by British organisations and establishments of family-friendly working practices and the determinants of the level of establishments' provisions. Chapter 3 examines employee entitlements to these arrangements. In Chapters 4 and 5 we begin to consider the effects of family-friendly policies on outcomes and workplace performance. Chapter 4 examines measures of employee commitment to see whether they depend, in any way, on family-friendly working arrangements; Chapter 5 considers employers' views on whether flexible family-friendly arrangements are costly, beneficial or value for money, and some of the business performance outcomes for British establishments. The conclusions are presented in Chapter 6.

2

Family-friendly arrangements in British establishments

There has been growing interest in which British employers offer family-friendly working arrangements to their employees. In this chapter we describe the analyses and results, using the newly available WERS dataset, on the question of which British employers had family-friendly working arrangements in 1998 and whether there were systematic reasons associated with offering employees certain types of working arrangement. Analyses using other data are not reported, for reasons described in Chapter 1.

Extent of family-friendly policies in Britain

Since the WERS data have been collected, the government has seen fit to carry out other surveys to provide statistical data on the extent of flexible and work–life balance practices and policies in British organisations in 2000. A comparison of the extent of the various practices from the latest sources, where they overlap, is provided in Table 1.

Table 1: Prevalence of flexible working patterns among British employers, by source and date

	% of employers in sample		
	WERS of employers 1998[b]	DfEE Work–life Balance Baseline Survey 2000[c,d]	DTI Employer Survey on support for working parents 2000[c,d]
Part time	82	88	77
Flexi-time[a]	27	25	32
Term-time only[a]	16	17	18
Job share[a]	27	24	21
Working from or at home	33	38 occasionally	18
Working from or at home[a] (non-managerial employees only)	13		
Ability to change from full- to part-time hours[a]	46		
Reduced hours		17	
Parental leave[a]	34		
Paternity leave (paid or unpaid)	48		18
Special leave for emergencies	24		
Unpaid leave for emergencies	18		
Annualised hours		8	
Compressed working week		7	

Notes:
[a] In the case of WERS data, on the question indicated, the availability of flexible working patterns is for non-managerial employees only.
[b] Sample: Establishments with 10+ employees.
[c] Sample: Establishments with 5+ employees.
[d] Source DTI (2000b).

Of the types of arrangement being considered in this report, the ability to change from full- to part-time hours had the highest frequency in 1998 for non-managerial employees. Working from home was the arrangement with the lowest frequency of employer provision for non-managerial workers, followed by term-time work. We suspect that the main differences in statistics between sources are related to the differences in samples and question definitions of the arrangements.

The numbers of family-friendly working arrangements are displayed in Table 2. Only around 14% of the sample did not have any of the nine arrangements. No establishments had all nine policies. Approximately 29% of establishments had four or more of these arrangements. This is a much larger proportion than was found in Forth et al (1997), but those authors asked about far fewer working arrangements than are counted here.

An analysis of the set of workplaces that did not have any family-friendly policies, compared with those who had at least one, revealed that the former had different characteristics from those in the majority group. Those without any policies were over-represented or far more likely to be:

- in manufacturing (27% compared with 12% in the with-policy group);
- in the construction sector (12% compared with 4% in the with-policy group);

Table 2: Number of family–friendly working arrangements in WERS establishments

Number of arrangements for non-managerial employees[a]	N	%
0	312	14.2
1	444	20.3
2	434	19.8
3	380	17.3
4	293	13.4
5	194	8.9
6	94	4.3
7	32	1.5
8	8	0.4
9	0	0
Total	2191	100

Note:
[a] One out of these nine, leave for emergencies, was not restricted to non-managerial employees. (Paternity leave and parental leave have been counted as one arrangement.)

- in establishments with up to 25 employees;
- in organisations with fewer than 500 employees.

Those workplaces without policies were less well represented in establishments:

- in the public sector (4% compared with 34% in the with-policy group) in all the various public sector categories, public authorities, education and health sectors;
- with over 200 employees;
- with a HR specialist (32% compared with 56% in the with-policy group);
- with a recognised union (28% compared with 59% in the with-policy group);
- with above average labour productivity (34% compared with 43% in the with-policy group);
- with recent bad industrial relations (12% compared with 21% in the with-policy group);
- with equal opportunities policies.

The absence rate was lower in the group that did not have any policies, and the percentage share of the workforce who were female was lower at 37% in the group without any policies than in the group with policies (51%).

Earlier studies

Until the availability of the WERS data, because of the lack of a suitable dataset, there were no British multivariate studies to explain which employers had flexible working arrangements. Since this research was started, a multivariate analysis of employers' uses of home working has been carried out using the WERS data by Felstead et al (2001a). The results are discussed alongside our own. There have been a greater number of US econometric studies, and US authors have developed the theory about the availability of flexible employment in organisations. Recently, Evans (2001) reported on a study from Australia in addition to employee evidence from the EU, the UK and the US.

Goodstein (1994), Ingram and Simons (1995) and Barringer and Milkovich (1998) are examples of US empirical studies on large-scale data aimed at testing hypotheses about whether organisations had provisions that addressed family–work challenges. A list of potential explanations was drawn up by these researchers. They are based on theories from economics and management studies about motivations and behaviour of employers and managers in the face of what are called institutional pressures, resource pressures, individuals' incentives (under the headings of agency and transaction costs) and cost or technical constraints. **Institutional pressures** are those that come from governments, interest groups or collective organisations. **Resource pressures** are constraints faced within organisations. **Individual incentives** to work hard (or not) present employers with decisions about the best way to structure rewards, payments systems, supervision and flexible provisions.

As well as the usual **costs** of labour, capital and other factors of production, theories have considered costs of information, monitoring workers' productivity, labour turnover and efficiency. This mixture of elements, some internal and some external to an organisation, have been summarised under two headings: institutional pressures, and expected efficiency gains (Barringer and Milkovich, 1998). The empirical work of Osterman (1995) linked the adoption of family–work programmes to pre-existing workforce problems, and to an organisation's use of high commitment work systems. However, Wood (1999) disputed this latter relationship using the same data. The analysis of the extent of workplace family-friendliness in the Australian Workplace Industrial Relations Survey (AWIRS) data from 1995 found that family-friendliness increased significantly with: average workplace weekly earnings; professional workers; clerical/sales workers; structured management; increases in employee numbers; having a written equal opportunities policy; and being in the public sector. Family-friendliness decreased as the percentage of non-core workers increased (cited in Evans, 2001).

Based on this literature and theoretical arguments, we expect that organisations are more likely to have family-friendly policies:

- when they experience or anticipate either institutional pressures from statutory legal enforcement, or bandwagon effects from demographic changes, pressure groups, unions or benchmarking with competitor companies: the public sector would be expected to

experience most pressure from the statutory environment;
- when resources in the organisation are favourable to their introduction, or key resources are lacking and could be procured through the introduction of flexible working arrangements. Hence, the following will all favour the introduction of family–friendly working arrangements: buoyant product markets, good financial or sales performance, and/or a specialist HR function that can help to administer and manage the flexibility. In larger establishments, skill shortages prohibit either further growth or the fulfilling of orders, which could be alleviated by using flexible working arrangements;
- when agency costs are reduced, for example where the costs of supervision can be lowered by allowing workers flexibility, and in conditions where reward incentives such as performance-related pay already perform the necessary control and supervision functions;
- where technical factors are favourable and there is a clear business case for having flexible working arrangements; through recruitment and retention benefits in situations of skill and labour shortages; and where there are few operational constraints to introducing the practice.

Approach adopted

We were interested to examine the determinants of whether an employer offered (non-managerial) employees an entitlement to particular types of working arrangement. All 10 of the set of family-friendly working arrangements in the WERS data listed in Chapter 1 were taken in turn. In addition, we attempted to explain the numbers of family-friendly policies organisations had adopted, out of a total on nine possible arrangements. The framework adopted was that of multivariate regression, as described in Chapter 1, where we set out to explain each employer decision to have (or not have) a particular working arrangement (or a number of them), with a set of potential explanatory measures that were available from the WERS data. Logistic regression was used to examine these dichotomous choice (zero/one) variables, and the ordered probit estimation technique was used in the case of explaining the number of arrangements each employer had.

The WERS data offered us measures of potential explanatory variables covering the employer's structural characteristics, workforce profile and HR policies (Table 3), linked to the type of explanation it might be providing. In some cases, research was required to derive some of the explanatory measures in advance of being able to use them to explain the employers' adoptions of family-friendly working arrangements. This was the case for the high commitment management approach, described in more detail below.

Determinants of working arrangements available

Institutional pressures

Our expectation that institutional pressures would make it more likely that organisations would adopt flexible working arrangements was largely supported by a number of different results. The public sector had the highest proportions of many of these working arrangements, but across the different public sector industry categories there was some variation in the size and significance of

Table 3: List of explanatory variables included and their theoretical interest

	Type of effect being captured
Structural characteristics	
Establishment size (set of banded categories used)	Resource
Organisation size (set of banded categories used)	Resource
Industry groups (set of categories used)	Technical
Foreign-owned	Institutional
Owner-controlled	Resource
Multinational	Resource
Recognised union	Institutional
Location of market (set of categories used)	Technical
Nature of competition (set of categories used)	Institutional
Percentage of labour to total costs (set of banded categories used)	Resource
Workforce profile	
Percentage of female to total workforce	Institutional
High proportion part time in female workforce	Institutional
Share of non-managerial/professional to total workforce	Agency
Has recruitment difficulties	Resource
Has policy to recruit female returners	Institutional/resource
Time taken to learn job (set of categories used)	Agency
High amount of discretion to learn main job	Agency
High proportion of temporary workers	Resource/agency
Human resource practices	
Family-friendly ethos	Institutional
Investors in People award	Institutional
Performance-related pay used	Agency
Other fringe benefits offered	Agency
Percentage on regular overtime	Resource/agency
HR specialist at the establishment	Resource
HR specialist at head office	Resource
Consults the workforce on equal opportunities and welfare	Institutional
Has equal opportunities policies (set of categories used)	Institutional
Industrial relations disputes in past year	Agency, transactions costs
High commitment management practices (HCM)	Institutional, resource, agency
Employer thinks employees are involved in decisions	Institutional, resource

Figure 1: Predicted probabilities for the public authorities sector

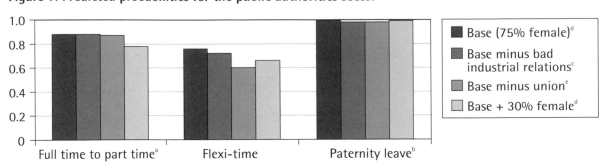

Note:
[a] Ability to change from full- to part-time hours.
[b] Availability of paternity leave scheme.
[c] Had industrial relations problems over the past year.
[d] Share of female to total workforce at establishment is 75% or 30%.
[e] Establishment does not have recognised union.
The base set of characteristics for these predicted probabilities of having a particular working arrangement are as follows: establishment size of 200–499 employees; in the public authorities sector; with a recognised union; local market competition missing; labour costs over 75% of total costs; two types of workplace change; 75% female workforce; high on part-time workers; 75% share of non-managerial workers; high on temporary staff; time to learn the job from one to six months; recruits returner females; has family-friendly ethos; Investors in People award; 30% do regular overtime; HR specialist in establishment; consults the workforce; equal opportunities implemented at high level of implementation of equal opportunities; and bad industrial relations recently; otherwise the reference category was used.

these sectors as determinants of having particular arrangements.

A selection of the predicted probabilities of having selected policies for the public authorities sector are displayed in Figure 1. These probabilities were much higher than those for other private sector establishments, as the later figures display. Being a public sector establishment in 1998 was not a relevant force in explaining why establishments had parental leave. This was before parental leave became a statutory arrangement. The public authority sector was influenced to offer paternity leave, term-time work, the ability to change from full- to part-time hours and flexi-time, but not home work. The lack of home working in public administration is perhaps not surprising, given the need to deal mainly with customer queries. This demonstrates the role that operational or technical constraints play in devising the type of flexible arrangements on offer, even within an environment in which there is a basic predisposition to respond to institutional pressures, as noted in Yeandle et al (2002: forthcoming).

Unions

The earlier US studies suggested that organisations were less likely to have flexible

arrangements where unions were present. This may be because of the nature of US organisations, with their low level of union representation outside of certain male manufacturing enclaves, and with employers offering fringe benefits as standard without union involvement. The British setting is somewhat different. In Britain there is more of a tradition of unions negotiating about working conditions across a range of industries. White collar workers and women in unions have been growth areas, and, although there has been a general decline in membership, unions are still strong in the public sector in Britain.

Our results show that workplaces with a recognised union were more likely to have adopted family-friendly working arrangements, especially those of parental leave, paternity leave, job share, flexi-time, workplace nursery and (to a lesser extent) emergency leave. Home work was the exception, where having a recognised union was not found to be significant in our results. Felstead et al (2001a) found that unions (but measured differently to our measure) had a negative effect on the availability of home working. Having a union had its greatest effects on the probability of the employer having flexi-time and paternity leave (see Figure 2).

All of the arrangements for which unions had a positive effect, with the exception of emergency leave, also had a higher incidence in the public

Figure 2: Predicted probabilities to illustrate high commitment management effects

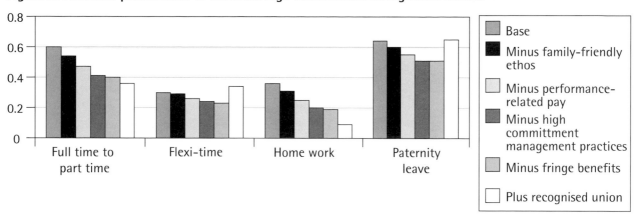

Note:
The base characteristics have items successively removed and the predicted probability recalculated to show the difference resulting from its removal.
The base characteristics for these predicted probabilities are as follows: an establishment of 200–499 employees; in business services; with few competitors; two types of workforce change; labour costs from 50–75% of total costs; 30% share of female workers; 30% share of non-managerial workers; time to learn the job six or more months; facing recruitment difficulties; a high amount of discretion in the job; a family-friendly ethos; performance-related pay; other fringe benefits; medium equal opportunities; high commitment management; and worker involvement in decision making; otherwise the reference category was used.

sector. We need to see the union presence in Britain, therefore, as a mechanism for reflecting and implementing institutional pressures in the public sector. However, separate estimations on private and public sector establishment samples found union influence to be significant and positive in both sectors, with the exception of job share, where the union did not have a significant effect on the likelihood of this arrangement being available in the private sector.

Female workforce

Flexible working arrangements were expected to be more likely to be available in workplaces with a higher proportion of women, through the pressures caused by demographic change in the composition of the workforce. These demographic changes have resulted in further institutional pressures as governments, especially in Europe, and interest group pressures have led over time to the introduction of new legislation. The introduction and enhancements of maternity leave and pay (and more recently parental leave) are clear examples of what has been a growing recognition of women's, and now men's, parenting responsibilities.

The expectation of a greater adoption of family-friendly policies where women are present also has its roots in the origin of such arrangements.

As we noted earlier, family-friendly working arrangements were originally devised in order to assist women workers. It is still the case that women, even when they are in full-time employment, are more likely than men to take responsibility for children and to seek certain types of flexibility in their working arrangements in order to fulfil those responsibilities (Dex, 1999). Survey data on women's and men's demand for flexibility shows that women are more likely to prefer options that reduce their hours of work (Hogarth et al, 2000).

Our results show that the extent of female employees is an important explanation in establishments' adoption of flexi-time, parental leave, job share, term-time working, the ability to change from full- to part-time hours and the provision of childcare and home work. In the case of job share and term-time work, this is also linked to working in the public sector and certain types of work in highly gender-segregated workplaces, such as schools. The adoption and use of flexi-time may be more related to the type of work being done; in particular, clerical and secretarial work have commonly been organised with ease using flexi-time. These, of course, are jobs dominated by female employees. Our own analysis of the WERS employees' data found significant correlations between having access to flexi-time and being a clerical worker (see Chapter 3 and Dex and Smith, 2001b).

Workplaces with a high proportion of part-timers in their female workforce exhibited a significant negative effect on the likelihood of having job share, childcare, home work and flexi-time provision. Part-time work and job shares are to some extent substitutes for each other, so this may explain why there is this negative relationship between the two. It is not surprising to see a negative effect of large amounts of part-time work on childcare. There is evidence from other sources that many women with children choose part-time work as a way on combining work and family life, and in order to minimise childcare costs (Dex, 1999). In workplaces with a high proportion of part-timers in the female workforce, the employer would probably experience and expect little employee demand for childcare provision or childcare assistance.

Human resources policies

Other representations of institutional pressures come from bandwagon effects from similar or competitor companies. In some cases, certain HR policies or fringe benefits become the norm, and companies feel pressured to adopt them to keep abreast of new developments and benchmarking. The concept of being *the* or *an* employer of choice is one that is often mentioned in company recruitment strategies since the 1990s, and clearly creates internal pressure to be parallel with or ahead in HR as well as other practices. High commitment management strategies may be another form of this kind of instituted HR pressure, as suggested in Osterman's (1995) research. Workforce involvement and consultation are part of a high commitment management approach. Companies with HR specialists are likely to be more able to address and respond to these pressures, but HR specialists are also a resource, without which it is difficult to introduce and implement new HR policies.

We found our measure of high commitment management practices to be associated with a higher probability of employers having the arrangements of home working, childcare help, parental leave, paternity leave, job share and the ability to change from full- to part-time hours. An additional measure of the extent to which the employer encouraged employees' involvement in the workplace was also significant in many of the same cases. Having a family-friendly ethos was significantly associated with offering parental leave, job shares, the ability to change from full- to part-time hours, home work and nursery provision. These results overlap, in part, with those of Felstead et al's (2001a, b) analysis of home working, as well as with Osterman's (1995) results for US employers.

A selection of the predicted probabilities of having these characteristics are displayed in Figure 2. The presence of a recognised union reversed the loss of a set of characteristics associated with high commitment management in the cases of flexi-time and paternity leave, but not in cases of home work or changing from full- to part-time hours.

Elements of what would generally be regarded as 'good employer' policies were also significant determinants of having family-friendly policies. Consulting the workforce on equal opportunities and welfare issues was associated with an increased likelihood of offering paternity leave. Having equal opportunities policies was a significant positive factor associated with flexible working arrangements in the case of all except emergency leave and, to a lesser extent, home work and flexi-time. It is also noticeable that more active pursuit of equal opportunities policies increased the probability of having the working arrangement in the cases where it had an effect.

The converse of being a good employer may be one for whom industrial disputes occur, and we might expect, therefore, a reduced likelihood of family-friendly policies being available in such a firm. However, our measure of recent industrial relations problems/incidents was associated with an increased likelihood of having the following working arrangements: childcare help, parental leave, paternity leave, job share and term-time working. These results may be mainly picking up the effects of industrial relations problems in unionised environments such as the public sector. It may be reflecting the fact that unionised workplaces have been subject to much reorganisation and increasing pressures over the last decade; but unions have helped to develop and implement family-friendly working arrangements in some contexts, as Bond et al (2002) have documented.

Competition

The extent of product (or service) market competition might influence the adoption of family-friendly working arrangements through the pressure of bandwagons. Having no competitors was associated with a firm's having parental leave, job share, flexi-time and emergency leave. Having a few competitors made it less likely that the employer would offer childcare help, or term-time work. We suspect that these results were partly a reflection of public sector workplaces.

Resource constraints

Size

We anticipated that flexible working arrangements would be more likely to be available in larger establishments and organisations (see Box 2). This relationship has been found in many earlier (mainly US) studies. Larger organisations will usually have the personnel or HR functions to implement flexible working arrangements; there may also be economies of scale factors in some cases, for example in providing workplace nurseries. Owner-controlled establishments tend to be smaller, in which case they may be less likely to offer flexible working arrangements. Multinational companies tend to be larger and might be expected, therefore, to be more likely to offer flexible working arrangements.

In our results, the size of establishment was not relevant to an employer providing parental leave or emergency leave; however, establishment size was an important factor associated with all the other flexible working arrangements we were able to consider. The positive relationship of home working with establishment size overlaps with that found by Felstead et al (2001a). A graded probability of having such a policy increased in steps as the size of establishments increased. The probability increased in large steps with establishment size, particularly in the cases of workplace nurseries and term-time work; the increases were relatively small steps in the cases of flexi-time, help with childcare and home work. A selection of the sizes of these effects is displayed in Figure 3 for three of the policies.

As the size of the organisation increased, holding establishment size constant, the probability of an employer offering parental leave, paternity leave, job share, term-time working, and the ability to change from full- to part-time hours also increased. However, organisation size was not relevant to the provision of a workplace nursery or home work. This is probably because the latter are arrangements that have to work at the establishment level, and so the size of the organisation is less relevant. The same reasoning probably applies in the cases of childcare help and emergency leave which also do not show a clear progression with organisation size, although the largest size of organisation (over 50,000 employees) did have a significant and higher probability than smaller organisations of offering these provisions.

Box 2: Establishments and organisations

An **establishment** is the term used for a particular workplace. It may or may not be the sole location of a particular employer's businesses activities.

An **organisation** may conduct its activities at a number of different establishments or workplaces. Organisations are potentially much larger than establishments.

There will be some employers for which the single establishment represents the full extent of the business activity. In this case, the establishment and the organisation are one.

Human resources specialists

The presence of a specialist HR function can be an important element of the resources available for HR policy development. We were able to include two measures, one relating to the establishment and one relating to a head office, where that applied. The result for the HR specialist at the establishment was significant in only three types of arrangement: as a positive effect on paternity leave, and as a negative effect on offering either home work or a workplace nursery. Perhaps HR specialists understand the nature of the costs of the nursery and would be loath to add administering this facility to their own workload. Having a specialist HR function at a head office was significant as a positive

Figure 3: Predicted probabilities of having a policy, by size of establishment (number of employees)

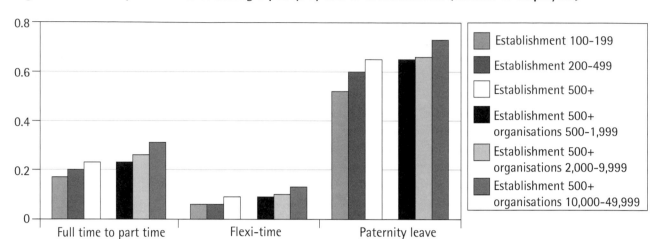

Note:
The base characteristics for these predicted probabilities are as follows: manufacturing establishment with a recognised union; few competitors; labour costs between 50% and 75% of total costs; two types of workforce change; 30% female labour force and 75% non-managerial to total workforce; the time to learn the job between one and six months; a percentage of workers doing regular overtime of 25%; and medium equal opportunities; otherwise the reference category was used.

influence in offering a range of working arrangements – in fact, all except nurseries and term-time work.

Good performance

It could be argued that, where the organisation is doing well, it will be predisposed to introduce more flexibility for employees. There is a long-established empirical link between pay and profitability. If family-friendly policies are seen as a form of fringe benefit, then better performance might be expected to lead to improved fringe benefits. Certainly there is case study evidence of the reverse relationship when financial services companies in Britain started to withdraw some of their flexible options during the recession of the early 1990s. If companies' main motivations for introducing flexible benefits was for business case reasons, we would not expect to see a relationship here. Having above-average financial performance in the private sector had a significant effect on offering all family-friendly arrangements except parental leave.

Market pressures

Flexible working arrangements were expected to be more likely to be available in certain industries, types of job and types of organisation. The constraints of competition vary by industry.

They are least in the public sector, and this is the sector where, as we mentioned earlier, institutional pressures to provide flexible working arrangements have been felt most.

In our results, industry categories had significant associations with some of the flexible working arrangements. Industry categories capture a range of dimensions of variation. At the broad level at which they were incorporated into these models, they capture some of the variations in product markets, labour market competition and variations between employers. But they also reflect some technical constraints relating to the nature of the product, the customers and the operations of production and management.

The manufacturing, utilities, construction and transport industries were less likely to offer all of the flexible arrangements or provisions under consideration. In these cases, the traditional male dominated industries and production lines have clearly not found the need or the way to offer flexible working arrangements or provisions to the same extent as other industries. Help with childcare was the one exception here, as the energy sector was more likely to offer this provision.

Outside of the public sector, positive industry associations were not common in this set of results. However, the hotel and catering sector was associated with term-time working; and business services was weakly associated with home working (as in Felstead et al, 2001a). The wholesale and retail sectors were associated with having paternity leave, and the financial services sector was associated with having flexi-time working.

Having recruitment difficulties at the time of the WERS, where significant, was more likely to lower the probability of a workplace offering flexible working arrangements (paternity leave, childcare assistance, and possibly flexi-time). Having a workplace nursery was the one arrangement that may have a positive association with recruitment difficulties. Employers who said they had a policy in place specifically to recruit female returners certainly had significant increased likelihoods of offering all of the arrangements under consideration, with only one exception – that of emergency leave.

Given that the data are cross-sectional, our results do not enable us to infer the direction of causation between these variables. However, it is likely that flexible working arrangements were introduced into such workplaces at least concurrently with a workforce strategy to recruit women with children. There is plenty of evidence of this type of employer behaviour (see for example Dex and Scheibl, 2002).

Supervision pressures and the nature of the work

We started out expecting that more highly qualified workers would be more likely to be allowed flexibility in their hours of work by their employers, who have to trust them to a greater extent to work flexibly in the workplace or at home. These are often workers who have received greater investment by their employers and certainly have cost more to recruit. They also have to fulfil more complex tasks, requiring initiative and discretion, which makes supervision more problematic. We were able to capture supervision pressures and the reward system through a number of variables.

The time taken to learn the job was associated with having certain types of flexible arrangement. Jobs that took the longest time to learn (more than six months), in comparison with the shortest time (less than one month), were associated with having flexi-time and parental leave. Jobs that

were medium (one to six months) in the length of time it took to master them were associated with job share and being allowed to change from full- to part-time hours; however, jobs with a medium learning time were less likely to be offered emergency leave. There is some evidence here, therefore, that more valuable workers, in whom employers have invested more training, are likely to be offered flexible working as a fringe benefit and retention incentive.

Employers who provided other fringe benefits were those who were more likely to allow working at home and the potential to change from full- to part-time hours. The higher the proportion of non-managerial workers in the establishment, the less likely the employer would be to offer either flexi-time, home work or paternity leave (overlapping with the Felstead et al, 2001a, b findings). A greater amount of discretion in the work carried out was also associated with an employer allowing flexi-time.

Less qualified workers were less likely to be allowed these arrangements. The fact that high proportions of part-time female employees made it less likely that the employer would offer flexi-time is further support for this relationship: part-time jobs in Britain are predominantly low skilled and low paid positions. The fact that a high proportion of temporary or fixed-term contracts in the workplace was associated with a higher chance of employers providing many of the flexible arrangements under consideration may seem to be counter evidence to this relationship. However, fixed-term contracts tend to be dominated mainly by professional workers, in which case the original conclusion gains further support.

Performance-related pay was positively associated with workplaces offering job share, changing from full- to part-time hours and working at home. This is a payment system that rewards output rather than inputs. It is not surprising, therefore, to find it correlated with working arrangements that also require a focus on outputs. Payment systems that relied on regular overtime for a large proportion of the workforce, not surprisingly, were often associated with workplaces where flexibility or other family-friendly provisions were not offered. This relationship may be capturing some traditional male dominated workplaces.

Technical and operations constraints

For some types of work, employers find it difficult to allow employees flexible working arrangements. Other studies have documented the constraints of meeting customer demands as well as production deadlines (Dex and Scheibl, 2002). Technical constraints were captured, to some extent, in our analysis by industry categories. Public sector industries (public authorities, education and health) would be expected to find it difficult to have home work provision since many involve delivering services at the workplace.

Our results suggested that being a public sector organisation was not a significant influence on the entitlement to home work provision. The fact that a large number of the other industry categories were significantly negatively associated with home working, and therefore less likely to offer it, is likely to be because of the technical and operations constraints of the business. For example, the business of manufacturing and construction usually needs to take place at the workplace or on site; the products and services for sale in wholesale and retail, and in the hotels and catering industries, for the most part need to be offered where the customers are located. The organisation of work has probably been changing substantially in the financial services, as the study in this Joseph Rowntree Foundation programme by Bond et al (2002) describes.

There is now more potential for working from home, assisted by new technology and telephone communications. However, in practice, many employers have moved to use the new technology in call centres that have more in common with manufacturing establishments. It is perhaps not surprising, therefore, that in these results the financial services sector was also associated with a lower likelihood of employers offering home work provision, after controlling for other factors.

Where the main market was international, there was a negative effect on offering flexi-time. That flexi-time was less likely in the case of international business may be related to the need to cover a wider range of trading hours across international time zones. Flexi-time might then pose problems.

Some of the other results also reflect constraints of the nature of the work. The education sector was less likely to have flexi-time, again, presumably because of the necessity of delivering the service during standard school hours. However, statistically significant increases in the likelihood of the provision were associated with the education sector and the availability of nurseries, emergency leave and term-time working. Education would be expected to be the sector, above all others, that would offer term-time working, so it is reassuring that the results confirmed this. The health sector had a higher probability of offering term-time only work and workplace nurseries.

Take up

Having a policy or practice is only one element of an organisation's involvement with work–family issues. The other side is whether and to what extent employees take up these policies and practices and, prior to that, whether they feel free to ask to benefit from them.

Information on take up in the WERS data is relatively thin. Certainly, more detail on this topic is provided in the more recent baseline work–life balance survey (Hogarth et al, 2000). In the WERS, those employers who gave non-managerial employees an entitlement to some sort of policy were asked what proportion of their employees had taken up any of these entitlements during the previous 12 months. The WERS data on take up of family-friendly working arrangements by employees was limited. Employers were asked about this, but not in a way that differentiated the different arrangements, except in the case of working at or from home.

The replies for the whole sample indicated that, for the vast majority of employers with some entitlement, only a small proportion had taken any of the entitlements, as indicated in Figure 4.

The highest usage of any entitlements over the previous year was found for establishments with a workplace nursery (94% had some usage; 17% had a quarter or more employees using an entitlement) and financial help for childcare (93% had some usage; 14% had a quarter or more employees using an entitlement). One contributing factor to the high usage of childcare

Figure 4: Employees who had taken any of the entitlements, from WERS – employers' information

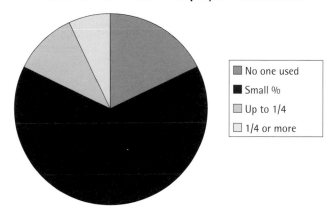

- No one used
- Small %
- Up to 1/4
- 1/4 or more

Conclusions

We found that the determinants of having family-friendly policies varied by the type of arrangement, but consisted of structural factors representing size of establishment, industry groups, operational constraints and the type of organisation, HR policies including worker representation and reward systems, and the workforce and type of job profiles. The findings of earlier surveys that did not use multivariate analysis were largely confirmed; that larger establishments, those in the public sector and unionised private sector establishments were important determinants of having family-friendly policies. However, our analysis also showed that the gender composition of the workforce was important in both sectors.

provisions is that employers who introduced workplace-based childcare will have assessed the demand for this provision before embarking on providing it, given its high cost. It is likely that the decision to provide childcare would have rested, at least in part, on there being sufficient employees who would use it. The lowest usage was in establishments offering the ability to change hours or parental leave (84% had some usage).

In the case of working at or from home, a separate question about usage of home workers in the establishment was asked later in the WERS questionnaire. In the total sample, 43% of establishments claimed to have some employees working at home some of the time, but for 39%, the reply was that "hardly any" or "a small proportion" of their employees used this arrangement. Only 4% of the whole sample allowed one tenth or more of their staff ever to work at home during normal working hours.

As indicated above, the percentage of WERS establishments claiming to use home workers was higher, at 43%, than the percentage of establishments saying that some non-managerial employees had an entitlement to work at or from home, at 18%. The gap is likely be due to the fact that managerial employees are included in the 43% whereas they are not in the 18%. These figures suggest that usage or take up of home working by British establishments who allow this practice is very small, and that entitlement is considerably greater for managerial employees than for non-managerial employees.

3

Employee access to family-friendly policies and practices

In this chapter we set out to examine the WERS employees' data in order to document which employees thought they had access to a range of family-friendly working arrangements. We examine the personal and job-related characteristics of these employees in order to get more understanding of employers' decisions about who they offer flexibility to.

However, it is one thing for employees to say that their employer allows particular working arrangements, and another to say that employees are necessarily correct in their perceptions of what is on offer. The potential mismatch between employers' policies and practices and what employees understand as their entitlements can create serious problems.

Unfortunately, because of constraints of space, we are not able to consider in this chapter all of the issues related to whether employees have a correct understanding of their employers' policies, or to present the analyses we carried out on this topic, although this is an important issue. We did find that there was a substantial amount of mismatch between employers' claims and employees' perceptions of their access to the various policies, more so in the cases of parental leave and leave for emergencies (see Dex et al, 2002). Here we will focus only on identifying and explaining which employees think they have access to these types of arrangement. The fact that there is an important amount of mismatch needs to be borne in mind in interpreting the results.

The extent of provision to employees

A large-scale employer survey in 1996 (Callender et al, 1997; Forth et al, 1997) found that part-time work was a non-standard working practice, available to two out of three mothers and used by two out of five, with 36% moving from full-time to part-time work when returning to their jobs after childbirth. One quarter of the returning mothers also reported that flexi-time was available to them, and one fifth of them had made use of it since the birth of their children. By contrast, only 12% of fathers had used this provision.

Entitlement to working flexible hours was available to two thirds of mothers in the public sector compared with one half in the private sector, and this was unrelated to the size of the organisation. Small private employers, with informal ways of working, were sometimes able to respond very positively to the need for flexibility (Forth et al, 1997).

The same survey noted that the convenience of working from home was available to just over one tenth of the mothers, with 8% reporting that they had worked from home at some time since their child was born. The proportion of fathers who had used this arrangement was about the same as for mothers. Large private establishments were more generous in allowing working from home than the public sector. This privilege was available to 48% of managers but to only 4% of women in protective and personal services. Similarly, men in higher grades were far more likely to be able to work at home than ordinary operatives or men working in personal and protective services. Felstead et al's (2001b) analysis of home working using the Labour Force Survey (LFS) found that home workers were more likely to be female, low paid, especially if women, in non-manual jobs, and women with children. Home workers were less likely to be from ethnic minority groups except if they were women, in which case they were more likely to be home workers.

The extent of WERS employee coverage by the various flexible working arrangements in 1998 is set out in Table 4. Since the WERS data were collected, the government has carried out another survey to provide statistical data on the extent of employees' access to flexible and work–life balance practices and policies in British organisations in 2000. A comparison of the extent of the various practices from recent sources, where they overlap, is also in Table 4. It is only the WERS data that are the subject of the analyses contained in this report.

Cully et al's (1999) analysis of the WERS data noted that public sector employers were, on the whole, more generous in all aspects of family-friendly employment benefits, including the provision of childcare subsidies (Table 5). In all respects, women beneficiaries outnumbered the men. However, the sad fact remained that almost a half (46%) of all employees received no such benefits. While the vast majority of employees were able to take time off to look after a sick child, most were obliged to use up paid leave, to make up for time lost or to forfeit pay for the time lost during the illness.

In some instances, this discrepancy between availability and use is due to better working conditions being offered to a privileged section of the workforce, in higher grades or selected departments (Thomson, 1995). A micro study of one company in the UK showed that managers were not even-handed in granting additional family or maternity leave or pay to their employees. They tended to regard family-friendly practices not as necessary supports, but as discretionary benefits (Lewis and Lewis, 1996). Forth et al (1997) found that, while between a quarter and a third of new mothers who were professional workers were entitled to a broad range of family-friendly arrangements, this applied only to 8% or 9% of those involved in sales and similar occupations. Job sharing, which usually involves splitting a full-time job between two people, was available to only one quarter of mothers and was used by less than one in ten.

There have been some recent multivariate analyses of a 1995/96 European Foundation source of EU employees with one child under 15 in the household, as reported in Evans (2001). On the employees' personal characteristics, women were more likely than men, employees working full time more likely than those working part time, and those with longer tenure more likely than those with shorter tenure to have access to the provisions. Evans concluded that the demand-side findings corresponded to those found in Australia and the UK; public sector firms or those with equal opportunities policies had the

Table 4: Prevalence of flexible working patterns among British and UK employees, by source and date

	% of employees in sample			
	WERS of employees 1998[a] (Britain)	LFS[b] (1998) (Felstead et al, 2000) (UK)	LFS[b] Spring 2000 (UK)	DfEE Work–life Balance Baseline Survey 2000[c] (Britain)
Part time	25		25	
Flexi-time	34		10	24
Term-time only			4	12
Job share	18		1	4
Working from or at home	11	Approximately 25[d]		
Parental leave	28			
Annualised hours				2
Compressed working week				6

Notes:
[a] Employees in workplaces with 10+ employees.
[b] LFS – Quarterly Labour Force Survey, UK.
[c] Employees in workplaces with 5+ employees, Britain.
[d] LFS has three questions covering the amounts of work at or from home. If aggregated they give the closest comparable definition to the less well defined questions in the other surveys.

Table 5: Access to flexible and family-friendly working arrangements, by sector and gender (% of employees)

	Private sector		Public sector	
	Men	Women	Men	Women
Flexi-time	24	36	37	39
Job sharing scheme	6	15	23	34
Parental leave	21	30	35	33
Working at or from home	10	6	13	9
Workplace nursery/child care subsidy	2	3	6	9
None of these	57	42	40	34

Notes:
Base: All employees in workplaces with 25 or more employees, Britain.
Figures are weighted and based on responses from 25,491 employees.
Source: Cully et al (1999)

most advantages. Professional, managerial and technician workers were more likely to report family leave benefits (except for sick leave) than craft, elementary, plant and machine workers.

Provision tended to increase with the size of the company. Of the industry sectors, financial services had the highest provision for their employees across Europe, with construction, retail and wholesale, and hotels and restaurant sectors being less likely to offer employees any of these provisions. Interestingly, the lowest company providers of the four types of provision by country were Scandinavian, presumably because the state is the main provider in these countries. Ireland, followed by the UK and Luxembourg, were the countries with the next lowest company providers of family-friendly arrangements. Austria, West Germany, Greece, Spain and Portugal most often had the highest levels of company provision. Until the availability of the WERS data, there were hardly any British multivariate studies to explain which employees had flexible working arrangements because of the lack of suitable data.

Approach adopted

As previously, we used a multivariate model to examine the determinants of whether an employee thought their employer offered them the availability of each of six types of working arrangement (listed in Chapter 1). A set of potential explanatory measures was available from the WERS data which consisted of the personal and job-related characteristics of the employees (Table 6), but also information, from the manager's questionnaire about the workplace (listed earlier in Table 3). Logistic regression was used to examine these dichotomous variables (has policy = 1, or 0 otherwise).

Table 6: List of explanatory variables included from employee questionnaire

Personal characteristics

Age
Sex
Health
Ethnic group
Marital status (measured with a set of categories)
Children and ages (measured with a set of banded age categories)
Educational qualifications (measured by one category, having a degree)
Recent training experience

Job related characteristics

Hours of work and overtime
Type of contract
Occupation (measured with a set of categories)
Amount of discretion in job
Views about how good employer is at communication and response to workers
Extent of managers consulting workforce
Job tenure (measured with a set of banded tenure categories)
Ethos of workplace
Union member and representation
Extent of sex segregation in workplace (measured with a set of categories)

The determinants of employees' access to provisions

The WERS data allowed us to investigate a number of hypotheses about the extent to which a range of employee and some employer characteristics explained employees' perceptions of their entitlements.

Employee personal characteristics

Employees' personal characteristics are likely to determine whether they have access to, and whether they are correct in *knowing* they have access to, certain employer provisions. Those with young children or other caring responsibilities, and women more than men, are the groups who have been the focus of the development of these policies. It is probable that workers in these traditional groups will be more likely to be offered such arrangements than those who are at different points in the life cycle. It is also probable that categories of workers who traditionally would have benefited will also be more aware of the benefits, partly from self-interest. Where there are larger numbers of potential beneficiaries, this too will aid the diffusion of information about the provisions. Those with ill health may have greater awareness of flexible working arrangements because of the necessity to use them. Ethnic minoritiy groups may be less likely to have access, or to be less well informed, if they are more marginal to the workplace or have suffered discrimination.

In our results, being female made it more likely that employees would have access to parental leave, job share, emergency leave and nursery and childcare subsidies. These results have overlaps with those of Evans (2001) for the EU as a whole. Women were less likely to have access to flexi-time and home working. Those with young children, especially preschool children, were also more likely to have access to most of these arrangements, including the provision of home working. However, again, this finding did not apply to the flexi-time working arrangement. In the case of parental leave, parents of children at all ages were more likely to think they had access to the provision than employees who did not have any children. While women and parents appeared to have better access than other groups, some types of arrangement fall outside of these

family-friendly developments, in particular, provision of home working and flexi-time.

Employees in poor health were no more (or less) likely to have access to these arrangements. The exception was flexi-time, where those with poor health were more likely than those in good health to have access to flexi-time working. Ethnic minority groups were less likely to have access to parental leave, but this result stood out from the rest. Whereas we had expected a negative effect on access from being in an ethnic minority group, only in the case of parental leave was this the case. Being a worker from an ethnic minority group made it more likely that access to flexi-time was available. For the rest, the relationships were statistically insignificant. Flexi-time is again singled out from the other provisions in this way.

We found that access to three of the provisions – parental leave, job share and childcare – declined with age, probably because of older workers having passed the relevant life cycle stage when these provisions were relevant. Only in the case of home working did access increase with age. We suspect this is a result of seniority, and the results on job duration partly support this. In the cases of parental leave, job share, emergency leave and, to a lesser extent, childcare and the provision of home working, the likelihood of access to the working arrangements all increased as job tenure increased. These relationships may also be related to internal organisation rules allowing employees access to certain provisions, as fringe benefits, after a certain period of tenure, or when trust has been established between employer and employee. However, the likelihood of working flexi-time decreased as job tenure increased.

One view of family-friendly provisions has been that they are additional fringe benefits to valuable employees, what is sometimes called the 'cherry picking' argument. In this case, from the employer's perspective, we would not expect that such provisions would be available to all employees equally. Employees with more firm-specific training embodied in them, and who were therefore more difficult to replace, would be expected to be more likely to be offered such fringe benefits. There may well be differences in provisions offered both within establishments as well as between establishments.

Workers with higher education, longer job tenure, full-time hours and permanent contracts would be also expected to know more about their employers' policies. Similarly, where employees feel their employer keeps them up to date and consults them about working arrangements, there is likely to be greater awareness of the provisions, and possibly greater provision resulting from employees requesting working arrangements that suit their responsibilities.

Our findings suggested that employees with a degree were more likely to have access to parental leave, job share, home work and childcare, but less likely to have access to emergency leave. This may be because higher qualified workers are more likely to have control over their working hours and be able to take time off for emergencies in a flexible way, without the provision of a specific employer scheme. The significant positive effect on access from having more discretion in one's job supports this view. Workers with a greater amount of discretion were all more likely to be offered parental leave, job share, flexi-time, home work and childcare, but were less likely to be offered emergency leave.

Employee job-related characteristics

There was some evidence, as found by Evans (2001), for the 'cherry picking' view in the way workers in the top occupations (professional/ managerial and associate professional), as well as those having received recent training, were often more likely than workers in craft skills, semi-skilled or unskilled job categories to have access to these flexible working arrangements. In this analysis of the WERS data, regarding parental leave, job share and flexi-time, clerical and secretarial workers had the highest likelihood of access to such working arrangements. This is probably related to the predominance of women in clerical and secretarial jobs and is evidence of the traditional female client groups still being the main beneficiaries of these provisions.

As we expected, those working part-time hours were less likely to have access to this set of flexible working arrangements. This may be partly through the lack of awareness of employers' provisions that working fewer hours implies. However, it is also likely to be because many part-timers will have already obtained the type of flexibility they wanted by working part

time and so will be less interested in other types of arrangement. Employees on temporary contracts were less likely to have access to parental leave or emergency leave, as we expected, but they were more likely to have access to childcare.

These results were unexpected, differing also from those of Evans (2001) for Europe. It may indicate that sectors that make more use of temporary staff are those more likely to offer some sort of childcare provision in Britain but not necessarily in the rest of Europe. The NHS would be one example where this relationship would apply.

Employees working regular overtime were less likely to have access to parental leave, job share, flexi-time, home working and childcare. However, regular overtime was associated with a greater likelihood of employers having emergency leave. These results are not surprising. If employees work regular overtime, this rather precludes flexi-time, job share and probably home working. In addition, regular overtime may be a feature of certain types of men's jobs. Working in a mainly male workplace made it less likely that employees would perceive that they had access to parental leave, job share, flexi-time or childcare.

However, it was not the case that working in a mainly women's workplace was associated with a greater likelihood of access to any of these working arrangements. Such an environment even made it less likely that home working or flexi-time arrangements would be available, although emergency leave was more likely in a female gender-segregated environment. This is probably because wholly women's workplaces are more often characterised by large amounts of part-time or low-waged jobs, and these often fail to offer their employees fringe benefits or flexible working arrangements (other than part-time work). These results mirror those found in the employers' data in Chapter 2.

Where employees considered their employer to have created a family-friendly ethos and reported that the workforce has been consulted, there were higher likelihoods of their having access to all provisions except emergency leave. In such environments, it may be that employers and employees were content for informal leave for emergencies to operate. Union membership for the employee was associated with a higher likelihood of access to four of the provisions; working at home and flexi-time were the two exceptions.

These results mirror those found in the employers' data in Chapter 2. However, an employee feeling represented in the workplace or being a representative only added an additional increased likelihood of access in the case of parental leave and job share. Unions have probably participated in negotiating entitlements to some of these provisions, and probably would also have improved the internal communications about the provisions available.

In addition to these more systematic relationships between employee characteristics and flexible working arrangements, we can see evidence of the constraints of certain jobs and working environments appearing through these results. Access to home working is perhaps the most obvious case where job constraints are probably influencing the results. Access to home working was progressively less likely as the skill of the job decreased. It is likely that lower skilled jobs need to be done in situ at the workplace to a greater extent than higher skilled jobs. However, it is also likely that employers do not trust those with fewer skills to work at home.

Those working in craft jobs were also regularly less likely to have access to these types of flexible working arrangements, but this is often in association with a wholly male working environment. It might mean, therefore, that traditional values and their associated working arrangements were part of the explanation. The higher likelihood of clerical/secretarial workers compared with other types of occupations working flexi-time has become a traditional working arrangement for such jobs, although it is undoubtedly founded on the fact that these sorts of support staff jobs can be organised in this flexible way.

In summary, we can see from the analysis of employee characteristics that access to these various flexible working arrangements can be characterised as follows.

- Access to parental leave and childcare are heavily characterised by life cycle factors of a predominantly female workforce of employees.

- Access to job share is also heavily characterised by life cycle factors, but also by clerical and secretarial work.
- Home working is a type of arrangement attached to certain types of men's jobs, as a fringe benefit or perk, and is reliant on seniority.
- Emergency leave is related to a predominantly female workforce at certain points in the family life cycle, but specifically at the lower ends of the skill and labour market status hierarchies.
- Flexi-time stands out from the other arrangements in being (a) less influenced by the pressure to accommodate family demands, (b) available to single people, and (c) more related to job characteristics of part-time work, overtime, having discretion but not necessarily being highly qualified, temporary, clerical/secretarial and gender-mixed environments.

Employer structural characteristics

Among the specific employer characteristics, size of establishment and size of organisation were important explanatory variables in the case of employees' access to parental leave, job share, nursery/childcare and flexi-time. The likelihood of access to these provisions, as found by Evans (2001) for Europe, tended to increase with establishment and organisation size except in the case of the nursery/childcare provision, which increased with establishment size but decreased with organisation size. Since there are heavy costs in setting up nursery provision, and it needs to be local to be effective for employees, it is not surprising that, as in the employers' data (Chapter 2), the weight of explanation is on the establishment size for access to nursery/childcare provision. It is not clear why this provision should be negatively related to organisation size instead of insignificant. However, it may be related to equity issues in the organisation. As organisation size increases, it may be less likely that any one (establishment) site would be offered this type of provision, since the costs for a larger organisation might prohibit it being offered to all.

Industry groups were relevant to these provisions, and industries appear to have favourite or clustered types of provision. Manufacturing appears less likely to offer job share and childcare, but more likely to offer emergency leave. This fits the employee profile we described above of lower level skill jobs being more likely to have access to emergency leave. Construction had a similar sort of profile. The wholesale/retail sector was less likely to offer job share, access to home working and childcare, but more likely to offer flexi-time. This is consistent with the nature of addressing customer needs in this sector. A similar type of profile applies to the hotel and catering industry, except that childcare provision was also more likely there. Financial services allowed access to home working and flexi-time but were not likely providers of childcare. Business services were also providers of home working and flexi-time with the addition of parental leave.

The public authorities sector was a more likely provider of all except childcare, although flexi-time was very prominent in the public authorities sector. In the education sector only childcare was more likely to be provided, with other provisions mostly less likely to be offered. The health sector was more likely to offer flexi-time, childcare and access to home working, but not parental leave or job share. These results are consistent with the known constraints of delivering services and products in these industries.

Working where there was a recognised union had a positive effect on access to parental leave, job share, childcare and flexi-time, overlapping with the employers' data in Chapter 2.

Owner-controlled workplaces were more likely than non-owner-controlled ones to offer employees access to parental leave, job share and flexi-time, but were less likely to offer emergency leave. Employers focusing on local markets tended to be associated with lower likelihoods of provision in comparison with regional markets, except in the case of job share. Similarly, an employer whose business was mainly in international markets was less likely to offer any of the provisions except emergency leave. The lack of competition was helpful in making job share and emergency leave available, but made it less likely for childcare, flexi-time, home work or parental leave to be offered. Labour costs had varying effects, with high labour intensity being associated with an increased chance of job share but a reduced likelihood of many other working arrangements. In these latter cases, it may be the skilled nature of the work that is being captured.

Employer workforce profile effects

Employers with a higher proportion of female employees were more likely to offer parental leave, job share and flexi-time, although these effects were often dampened by a negative effect of having a high percentage share of part-time workers in the female workforce, an effect that was fairly ubiquitous, as found in the employers' data in Chapter 2. A higher share of non-managerial workers and recruitment difficulties had the same negative effect across most working arrangements. This suggests that, rather than skill shortages encouraging employers to be more flexible, the pressures this created made it less likely that innovative solutions would be found.

Case study evidence supported this conclusion in the case of some small- and medium-sized enterprises (SMEs) (Dex and Scheibl, 2002). However, where female returners were specifically being targeted for recruitment, there was a greater likelihood of parental leave, job share, childcare and flexi-time (but not emergency leave) being offered. Also, where high proportions of temporary staff were employed, there was more likelihood of all family-friendly arrangements being available with the exception of job share. This may mean that, in situations where temporary staff have been used to solve the recruitment problems, family-friendly working arrangements can be introduced. Alternatively, it may mean that family-friendly working arrangements are more likely in settings where temporary staff are integral to the work being carried out and are not part of a strategy to deal with a crisis in recruitment or organisation change. This distinction between different approaches to the use of temporary workers was seen in a set of employer case studies (Dex et al, 2000).

Employer human resource policy effects

The high commitment management theories have argued that this type of approach has the potential to get greater commitment from employees, as they feel more involved in the production process and are encouraged to improve it. We might expect that employers who adopted such approaches would be more likely to communicate effectively with their employees and offer them customised benefits to meet their caring and personal responsibilities. Arguments of this kind have been examined in the literature (Osterman, 1995; Wood, 1999). Certainly, we would expect employers who saw themselves as having a family-friendly ethos to be more likely to offer family-friendly working arrangements to their employees.

Human resources policies were related to the level of family-friendly provision in a number of ways. A family-friendly ethos led to a higher likelihood of provision of parental leave, job share, childcare and flexi-time. Where employers offered other fringe benefits they were more likely to reduce the likelihood of provision, presumably because the other fringe benefits acted as substitutes for any spending or costs associated with family-friendly provisions. Having the resources of an HR specialist on site helped in offering parental leave, job share and childcare; an HR specialist at head office helped in the case of home working.

Workplaces with equal opportunities policies, especially where the implementation was at a high level, were more likely to offer a range of family-friendly arrangements, as found in Evans' (2001) analysis of European employees. Also, workplaces with a bad industrial relations record were more likely than other workplaces to offer a range of provisions. It may be that the industrial relations incidents had encouraged establishments to offer family-friendly provisions to restore the psychological contract in the way Bevan et al (1997) suggested. Alternatively, industrial relations incidents may be more a feature of union activism, which has also been shown to be associated with greater provision of family-friendly working arrangements.

Employers who consulted with the workforce about equal opportunities and other welfare issues were more likely to give access to parental leave and emergency leave. This is interesting in that, at the time of the WERS (when there were no statutory days of leave available for family reasons), research indicated that women's top priority for things that would improve working conditions was days of leave to cope with emergencies (Bryson et al, 1999). It looks as if the process of consultation may have uncovered this desire in workplaces where it occurred.

The adoption of high commitment management strategies was associated with an increased likelihood of provision of childcare and flexi-time.

Management that considered itself to involve employees was also associated with greater provision of flexi-time. This does not suggest a large role for high commitment management approaches in the development of family-friendly working arrangements. This is an area where the employees' results differed from those found for employers in Chapter 2. However, some of the strong industry effects, and some of the other HR policies, may also be reflecting differences in HR approaches that overlap with high commitment management strategies.

Conclusions

The profiles of the employees who had access to various types of family-friendly provisions make a lot of intuitive sense. The main dimensions of explanation revealed in these results were that employees' access to flexible provisions was determined by a mixture of:

- the (female) gender of the worker;
- the childcare responsibilities;
- traditional values as reflected in gender working groups;
- the constraints of the job;
- the potential for flexibility in the job without particular arrangements being needed;
- fringe benefits resting on seniority and trust; and
- some 'cherry picking'.

The examination of employees' characteristics showed a certain amount of overlap with the employer profiles found in Chapter 2. The workforce gender profile, the process of consultation and the role of the unions were common parts of the explanation. The type of workplace offering flexi-time and emergency leave differed from that offering other types of family-friendly working arrangements in ways that mirrored the employer characteristics that were found to be important. However, we should also remember that emergency leave had one of the lowest levels of agreement about the provision between employee and employer.

Strong workplace predictors of access were found in the sizes of establishments, the industry sector, and elements of the HR strategy and policies. To a large extent, these overlapped with Evans' 1995/96 results from a sample of EU employees (Evans, 2001).

4

Employee commitment as an outcome

There has been considerable policy interest in whether family-friendly policies or flexible working arrangements have business benefits, the so-called 'business case'. If there are demonstrable benefits, then policy makers have a persuasive instrument with which to approach employers. The potential benefits considered in this discussion include measures of employer or business performance, the *hard end* of benefits. Under this heading fall productivity increases, financial performance, or employee turnover and absenteeism reductions, or recruitment and retention benefits. These are considered in Chapter 5. At the *soft end* of benefits come employee morale, employee attitudes and employee commitment. The soft-end benefits are thought to produce, in due course, hard-end benefits.

In this chapter we are interested in whether family-friendly practices affect employee commitment as an outcome. In this sense, its importance is as an intermediate outcome. However, whether employee commitment does feed through into the hoped-for performance benefits is not proven, and poses serious methodological challenges to address (Guest et al, 2000b).

Clearly, employee commitment is a complex concept. Researchers have debated the nature of this concept, and empirical studies have examined the links between commitment and other outcomes, and between commitment and the antecedents of management and supervision styles. While commentators have suggested favourable links between work–life balance policies and employees' commitment to the organisation (and ultimately to business performance), there has been relatively little evidence about these relationships. This chapter

sets out to examine the more limited issue of whether family-friendly working arrangements affect employees' commitment.

Literature on employee commitment

There is a large literature on workers' commitment and its determinants. Our technical paper (Dex and Smith, 2001c) covers the main points of the determinants of worker commitment as revealed in other studies. These earlier findings were used to inform our derivation of control variables in the analyses we undertook. We focus here, for background, solely on the literature relating to the effects on worker commitment of work–life balance policies.

In addition to indirect evidence of a link between commitment and work–life balance policies, more direct links have been noted based on workplace experiments. Early reviews of the studies measuring the effects on flexi-time and compressed working week arrangements on employee attitudes found that the introduction of these arrangements had uniformly positive effects (Golembiewski and Proehl, 1978, 1980; Neuman et al, 1989). However, in general there are criticisms of the lack of rigour in the design and in the measures used to evaluate interventions (Gottlieb et al, 1998). The effects on job satisfaction have been found to vary between positive or no effects (Gottlieb et al, 1998). Canadian studies cited in Gottlieb et al (1998) found that telecommuters reported higher commitment to the organisation than other workers, and both telecommuters and part-time workers had lower levels of intention to seek a new job. Unlike some of the other outcomes measures (stress, work–life balance, productivity) investigated by Gottlieb et al, whose results varied according to whether employees had a choice about their working arrangements, attitude or morale effects were found not to be influenced by the choice element.

Interviews with the managers in 83 organisations that had some family-friendly arrangements (IRS, 2000) found that 68% of these managers thought that commitment and/or motivation increased as a result of having family-friendly policies. Similar percentages of managers also thought that employee relations and job satisfaction improved for the same reasons. AON Consulting (2000) suggested that the lack of work–life balance in companies' agendas, along with stress, dissatisfaction with rewards and poor management of change, were the drivers of low commitment in organisations.

Guest et al (2000a, b) investigated whether it was more likely to be bundles of practices, rather than particular practices in isolation, that would affect employees' and performance outcomes more generally. They could not find evidence that bundles of practices were important.

Measures of employee commitment

The many research studies that have focused on work commitment have served to uncover the complexity of this concept to the extent that authors have characterised it as having no stable meaning (Becker, 1964), elusive meaning (Guest, 1992) and pluralist meaning (Morrow, 1983; Coopey and Hartley, 1991; Healey, 1999). Morrow identified 25 forms of commitment, although they were able to be reduced to five main foci: value, career, job, organisation or union focus. There other forms of job-related commitment, for example to clients or customers, visible in some public service institutions.

The focus of our interest has to be on organisational commitment. Even under this heading, there are alternative angles on an employee's organisational commitment, for example task commitment (to see the job through), continuance commitment (to stay in the organisation), normative or affective commitment (feelings of loyalty or shared values with the organisation), financial commitment (to the

material rewards) or temporal commitment (to a certain amount of work).

Gallie and White (1993) measured employee commitment to paid work from a 1990 survey and found that it was relatively high in the workforce as a whole and appeared to have increased compared with 15 years earlier. There was little difference between men and women. Only one third of employees exhibited high involvement in their current job, that is, **task commitment**. A recent consultancy report by AON (2000) claimed, from a survey of 1,570 workers, that 39% of UK workers were committed to continuing in their jobs, that is, **continuance commitment**.

There was a limited choice in the WERS data for devising a measure of employee commitment. The measure we used focuses on the employee's view rather than the employer's, bearing in mind that these two may differ. It is closest to the notion of **affective or normative commitment** described in the literature.

In each case, employees were asked to score the following statements, each scaled from 1, strongly disagree, to 5, strongly agree:

- "I share many of the values of my organisation."
- "I feel loyal to my organisation."
- "I am proud to tell people who I work for."

By summing these scores, a scale from 3 to 15 was constructed which passed the normal tests for reliability. On this composite scale, employees (N=26,115) could be classified as follows:

- 16% had low commitment (scores 3 to 8)
- 42% had medium commitment (scores 9 to 11)
- 42% had high commitment (scores 12 to 15).

Approach

As previously, we used multivariate analysis to examine the determinants of our measure of employee commitment. We were interested in whether family-friendly practices (or their number) were associated with higher levels of employee commitment. The question of whether higher commitment is produced or caused from more flexible working arrangements being offered to employees has to be left to further study using longitudinal data.

One novel feature of the data is that we had information about family-friendly working arrangements from two sources: from the manager's questionnaire, and, for a smaller set of arrangements, from the employee's perceptions. We were therefore able to examine both sets of arrangements and compare the results to see if the source of the information makes any difference to the conclusions.

In examining whether flexible working arrangements contributed to explaining employees' commitment, we needed to make sure that we did not identify spurious relationships because we had missed out other intervening and correlated variables. A set of other potential explanatory measures were available from the WERS to use as controls. These consisted of the personal and job-related characteristics of the employees (Chapter 3, Table 6), but also information from the manager's questionnaire about the workplace (listed in Chapter 2, Table 3). Ordinary least squares regression was used to examine a transformed (log) measure of employee commitment.

Determinants of commitment

The literature points out that a range of personal characteristics would be expected to affect worker commitment. In addition, we expected that employers' HR policies as well as, possibly, other structural characteristics about the workplace would be likely to affect employee commitment. These factors were also examined in detail.

Family-friendly policy effects: employers' information

After controlling for other potential determinants, there were positive effects from family-friendly policies where they were offered in the private sector, and more negative effects where they were offered in the public sector. In the private sector, having a workplace nursery, offering help with childcare or allowing employees to work at home were associated with higher employee commitment. The number of policies was insignificant in the results reported, although we did estimate some models on the private sector sample where the number of policies had a significant and positive effect on commitment. The sizes of the effects were all very small in comparison with some of the other control variables, ranging between 1% and 4% on the log scale from the presence of the arrangement.

In the public sector, significant negative effects on employee commitment were associated with employers offering job share, the ability to change from full- to part-time work, flexi-time, a workplace nursery, emergency leave, home work and with a higher number of policies overall.

We also examined whether other correlated variables were capturing some of the effects on family-friendly policies and thus weakening their coefficient sizes and significance. The idea that organisations adopt policy bundles, as Guest (1997) considered, was also a factor to consider. In neither case did we find evidence of these alternative effects.

Family-friendly policy effects: employees' information

Making use of the information provided by employees led to some differences in the results. In the total employee sample, where policies overlapped, the direction of the effects (increasing or decreasing) were similar to those from employers' information, but the significance varied. Employees who thought their employers offered parental leave (non-statutory), job share, flexi-time or a higher number of policies all tended to have lower levels of employee commitment than employees who did not believe they were offered such arrangements.

In the private sector sample, job share retained its significant negative effect on commitment, but being able to work at home had a significant positive effect on commitment. The predominance of negative effects from family-friendly policies was again evident in the public sector estimations using employees' information; in all public sector cases other than emergency leave, which did not have a significant effect, the effects of employees perceiving their employer to offer family-friendly policies was negative.

These public sector results certainly came as a surprise to us. Attempts to explore and explain these differences by incorporating interaction terms did not uncover any obvious statistical reasons for these effects. It is clear that it is not the lack of knowledge by employees of their employers' policies that is the explanation, since the same effects are visible in estimations using employers' and employees' information.

We cannot eliminate the possibility that reverse causality explains this effect, and that organisations with lower employee commitment have introduced family-friendly policies as a way of trying to address their problems. These effects remain, therefore, largely unexplained, although we found we were not alone in finding adverse results for the public sector from the WERS data (see Guest et al, 2000b). Lapido et al (1999) noted low commitment from midwives to their organisations but high commitment to their clients.

In the end, we can only speculate about why this might be the case. There may be a failure to implement these provisions, even though family-friendly policies are clearly more extensive in the public sector. If this type of window dressing has been occurring, it may have made employees cynical. A workplace culture that militates against take up might also have this effect. It might be that family-friendly provisions cause increased disruption and bad feeling in a hard-pressed public services environment if there is no cover for absence. Further research is needed to clarify this relationship.

Where the employer thought there was a family-friendly ethos in the establishment, there was a significant association, in the whole sample of employees – but not in the non-managerial sub-sample – with lower employee commitment. The private sector results did not reach significance and the variable for the public sector had insufficient variation to be incorporated. However, the employee's perception of the ethos of the organisation was systematically important across private and public sectors. Being thought by employees to be a more family-friendly organisation was associated with higher employee commitment, an effect of around 4% on the log commitment scale.

Controlling variable effects

Significant effects were found from control variables capturing individuals' personal characteristics, their job-related characteristics, organisations' HR policies and structural characteristics of the organisation. The employee job-related characteristics were by far the strongest determinants of employee commitment; in particular, their job satisfaction, their view of the management and being in a professional or managerial job (although only in the private sector) had the largest influences on commitment.

Conclusions

The effects of family-friendly policies have been found to be relatively small compared with other predictors of employee commitment. Nonetheless, after a whole array of controlling variables about employees, family-friendly policies relating to childcare and working at home have been found to improve employee commitment in private sector establishments. The fact that other control variables play a bigger part in explaining employee commitment does not detract from the importance of our findings for family-friendly policies.

An explanation for the poorer record of commitment for the public sector is not possible within the context of this study, although statistical anomalies have been ruled out as an explanation for these sectoral differences. Where employees, but not the employer, thought the organisation had a caring ethos, it was found to be an important determinant of increased employee commitment.

5

The business case for having family-friendly policies

Whether organisations that have family-friendly policies perform better than those who do not have such policies and practices is an important issue. This 'business case for flexibility' is being discussed by policy makers who want to advocate flexible working arrangements in companies and by academics.

The suggestion is that the costs of introducing flexible working arrangements are far outweighed by the potential benefits. The evidence on the business case up to the late 1990s was assembled in a number of documents covering US econometrics studies and case studies from Britain and the US.

Up to 1998, Britain, unlike the US, lacked appropriate large-scale survey data to use to model the determinants of performance and examine the effects of family-friendly policies. We have now had the opportunity to examine this question using the WERS data and another data source, collected from and collated about the FTSE100 companies in 1998. This was an important opportunity for a British statistical examination of these issues. We concentrate in this chapter on examining the business case arguments using the WERS data, having explored outcomes such as employee commitment earlier in Chapter 4. The analyses we undertook of the FTSE100 data are reported in the Appendix.

Business case literature

The 1996 PSI study reported that equal numbers of British employers saw advantages and disadvantages in providing family-friendly working arrangements (Forth et al, 1997). Employers were most likely to perceive benefits for improved staff morale and loyalty together with improved staff relations. The main disadvantages related to increased administration and the disruption through having to cope with staff absences (Forth et al, 1997).

There is a general literature on the determinants of workplace performance as well as more focused reviews of the effects that HR practices have on performance. Here, we summarise the main findings of the review of HR and flexible working arrangements on business performance. We are unable to cover the much wider literature on the determinants of performance in general.

Richardson and Thompson (1999) reviewed the studies of the effects on performance of HR practices. They noted that different researchers used quite different measures of HR practices and strategies. In addition, a range of performance measures have also been used. Not surprisingly, studies have often reached different conclusions. This is an area fraught with conceptual difficulties and challenges, therefore. On the whole, firms scoring high on what Richardson and Thompson called 'investment employment practices' (for example benefits, training, supervision) appeared more successful than those using 'contractual employment practices' (for example hiring strategies, flexi-time, part-time work, labour costs), although firms scoring well on both also tended to have higher labour productivity.

A number of potential effects on performance have been noted in this case study literature; notably, improvements in turnover, retention, absenteeism and productivity as well as morale (Bevan et al, 1999; Dex and Scheibl, 1999). In some cases, precise measures have been carried out; in other cases, managers' perceptions are the basis for the claimed improvements. Earlier

British case studies have not carried out controlled comparisons, although some US studies of the effects of introducing flexi-time have had control groups. In the US, case study material on the flexibility issue is also supplemented by company experiments (Bailyn et al, 1998). A smaller number of US econometric studies have found evidence of productivity increases associated with flexible working arrangements in a survey of US companies (for example Shepard et al, 1996).

The first analyses of the 1998 FTSE100 data (Winter, 1999) suggested that companies rated 'very good' on a range of equal opportunities and family-friendly provisions had a higher than average FTSE100 share performance for the five years up to 1978 than those who did not have these policies. The chronological timing of these data mean that we cannot be sure that better performance has resulted from having the policies.

The IPD's (Institute of Personnel and Development) (2000) survey of HR professionals about employee absence in their organisations found that it varied by region, and by the size of the organisation. HR professionals also reported that they thought that family-friendly policies had an effect in reducing absence.

The CIPD (Chartered Institute of Personnel and Development) (2000) survey of labour turnover, as reported by HR survey respondents, found that labour turnover varied by occupation group and industry, and declined with organisation size for full-time but not for part-time employees, who mostly had higher turnover at all sizes of organisation. Huselid (1995) among others found that high commitment management affected turnover.

Since the WERS 1998 data became available and while this project was in progress, several studies have examined the performance measures available in the data (Perotin and Robinson, 1999; Turner, 1999; Guest et al, 2000a). These studies have not focused on the effects of flexible working practices, although in some cases variables capturing family-friendly policies, or those that might be expected to be correlated with family-friendly arrangements, have been entered as explanatory variables. The number of family-friendly arrangements out of seven was not found to be a significant determinant of labour productivity by Perotin and Robinson (1999),

although having equal opportunities policies was associated with above-average self-assessments of labour productivity. A full review of the findings from the other studies can be found in our technical paper associated with this topic (Dex et al, 2001).

Costs and family-friendly policies in the WERS

The WERS data provided the opportunity to investigate perceptions of costs and benefits further on a larger sample. Unfortunately, the WERS questions covered both costs and benefits in an undifferentiated way across all the arrangements. This means that there is far less scope for analysis of these questions.

Managers in WERS establishments were asked questions that were pre-coded about the costs associated with giving their non-managerial employees entitlements to family-friendly working arrangements. These questions were asked of those employers that had at least some level of take up of the practices (as a whole) by their non-managerial employees. However, the questions about costs were not linked to specific establishment policies.

Eighteen per cent of establishments stating that employees had entitlement to at least one family-friendly policy also responded that none of their employees had taken any of the entitlements during the previous 12 months (13% of the total sample of establishments).

Managers' views about the costs of policies are set out in Figure 5. Although we were unable to link provisions and cost responses directly, it was clear that those who said they offered entitlements to workplace or other nurseries, or gave financial help for childcare, were much more likely to say that there had been moderate or substantial costs associated with policies. Approximately one third of establishments with either of these two provisions said they had incurred additional costs (moderate or substantial) for their establishment. This is not surprising and is what we might expect from this list of policies. An indication that there had been costs associated with the entitlements was lowest among establishments that said they offered a switch from full- to part-time employment.

Figure 5: Managers' views about the costs of flexible working arrangements, from the WERS

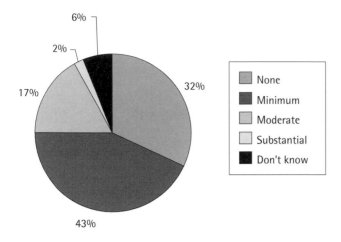

Legend:
- None
- Minimum
- Moderate
- Substantial
- Don't know

Determinants of being costly

The WERS data allowed us to examine, using multivariate analysis, which characteristics were associated with managers' perceptions that family-friendly policies were costly.

Being costly, in this context, was defined as meaning that there were either substantial or moderate additional costs associated with providing one or more of the entitlements. This measure of being costly was turned into a dichotomous variable (1 = costly, 0 otherwise) and estimated using a logistic regression. A set of potential explanatory variables was derived from the manager's questionnaire and used to explain whether entitlements to family-friendly policies were *thought to be costly*. A subset of structural characteristics, workforce profile, HR and performance measures were used from the list in Tables 3 and 7.

The likelihood of family-friendly entitlements being seen as costly was found to *increase* in establishments with:

- a workplace nursery
- help with the costs of childcare
- larger proportions of employees having taken up the provision in the last year
- owner control
- fewer than 500 employees
- above-average labour productivity
- below-average financial productivity.

Some further analysis of the determinants of being costly was carried out. This was to take into account that, in considering costs of family-friendly policies, we were considering only a selection of the companies, that is, those that had at least one family-friendly practice and had experienced some take up. (The WERS questions on costs were addressed only to this group.) It might be the case that employers who actually offered family-friendly policies were those that found them less costly, and that this influenced their decision to adopt them in the first place. Alternatively, having direct experience of these policies may have made employers more realistic about the costs (either more, the same or less than they expected) compared with employers who did not have any experience. Some of the variables found significant in the earlier analysis, therefore, may be partly capturing the effects of having a family-friendly entitlement compared with not having any entitlements. Since this may be related to viewing the arrangements as costly, we adopted a statistical procedure that would allow for this interference.

The results merely reinforced the earlier conclusions. The dominant effects explaining whether companies found their policies costly were: using a workplace nursery, giving help with the costs of childcare, and higher levels of take up. Since our data were cross-sectional, at one point in time, we cannot infer causal relationships from these results.

Types of benefit considered in the WERS

Managers in WERS establishments were asked open-ended questions about the benefits resulting from any non-managerial employees having an entitlement to family-friendly practices, in circumstances where at least some employees had taken any of the entitlement during the last 12 months. Some respondents gave more than one answer.

Of the establishments represented,

- 50% replied that they had happier employees;
- 21% said that the entitlement had increased workplace performance;
- 38% said it had helped with retention of employees; and

- 4% said it had made it easier to attract or recruit new employees.

Those employers with the entitlement of parental leave and working at home were more likely than the average to think they had happier staff.

Those employers allowing working at home or term-time work were more likely than the average to think they benefited from increased workplace performance.

Those employers providing nurseries were less likely than the average to think they benefited from increased workplace performance.

Those employers offering job share, nurseries or financial help with childcare were far more likely than the average to think they benefited from retention of employees.

Those employers offering nurseries or financial help with childcare were far more likely than the average to think they benefited from it being easier to attract and recruit new workers.

The net balance sheet

Of the same sample that had at least one entitlement and had employees who had used it, 87% thought the entitlements had been cost effective.

Very high proportions of relevant employers (92%) that permitted working from home or term-time work thought that their entitlements (as a whole) were cost effective.

Of those establishments thinking that their nursery provision had involved substantial costs, two thirds felt it was cost effective and one third that it was not. Similar proportions of those who thought their financial help with childcare involved costs replied that it had been cost effective (or not).

WERS performance measures

A number of organisation performance measures were available in the WERS manager questionnaire:

"I want to ask you how your workplace is currently performing compared with other establishments in the same industry.

How would you assess your workplace's

– financial performance?

– labour productivity?

– quality of product or service?"

The coded responses consisted of a five-point scale, in each case, ranging from "a lot better than average" to "a lot below average". We do not have any authenticating data for these managers' perceptions of the organisation's performance. One might expect that, if anything, managers would tend to exaggerate their firm's performance. The results suggest that this may have occurred. All of these questions tended to elicit what is probably a bias towards positive reporting of performance, as Table 7 illustrates.

Establishments were also asked about the value of their sales over the previous 12 months and whether they were rising (55% of establishments said yes), falling (13%) or stable (32%). We constructed another dichotomous performance measure from these responses, with 1 indicating rising sales (0 otherwise).

Estimations were carried out on these four measures for the private sector organisations only, since the questions were not thought to be relevant to most public or voluntary sector establishments.

Two additional workforce or HR performance variables were also analysed, since these have been central to the business case discussions about the effects of family-friendly policies:

1. the days of absence (number of workdays lost through employee sickness or absence not authorised) over the previous 12 months (with a mean of 4.4 days);
2. labour turnover: calculated as a ratio of the total number of leavers during the previous 12 months to employees in employment at the time of the survey (with a mean of 20.8%).

Since these variables were relevant to both private and public sector establishments, estimations of the models were carried out on the

Table 7: Summary descriptive statistics on the WERS performance measures (weighted) (%)

Assessment	Financial performance		Labour productivity		Quality of product service	
	All establishments	Private sector	All establishments	Private sector	All establishments	Private sector
A lot better than average	12.8	14.5	10.4	11.0	23.1	26.0
A little better than average	35.8	37.9	32.7	32.3	47.4	48.2
About average for industry	31.5	31.0	36.1	39.3	19.7	18.0
Below or a lot below average	6.4	6.5	3.6	3.8	1.9	1.6
No comparison or not relevant data	13.5	10.1	17.2	13.6	7.8	6.2
Total %	100	100	100	100	100	100
N	2,163	1,632	2,143	1,618	2,166	1,633
Missing	34	15	50	29	24	16

private sector sample as well as on the whole sample of establishments.

Some further comment needs to be made about the absence statistics. For purposes of contributing to the work–life debate, this measure is not ideal since it conflates two concepts: sickness (which can be a genuine and necessary reason for missing work) and absenteeism (which is when employees have time off for reasons that are not recognised as valid by their employer). Of course, both sickness and absenteeism may increase where work–life is not in balance.

Also, in practice, these two things are difficult to separate. In the IPD (2000) survey of absence, HR managers estimated that one third of sickness absence was not the result of ill-health. However, the conflation of these two concepts in one statistic is not ideal. While there may be some overlaps, we would expect different sets of factors to influence sickness and absenteeism. Of the performance measures available in the WERS, this statistic is the most problematic, therefore, and should be treated with the most caution.

The approach adopted

As previously, we carried out multivariate analyses to identify the determinants of establishment performance. We were interested in whether family-friendly practices (or their number) as revealed in the employer's data were associated with increased performance. An ideal test of these relationships should introduce a time dimension in which the policies and

characteristics of the organisations are lagged in time before the subsequent performance. Our data were merely a cross-section, with the implication that we have to leave to further study, using longitudinal data, the question of whether offering such working arrangements to employees leads to improved performance.

What we had to make sure was that we did not identify spurious relationships because we had missed out other intervening and correlated variables. A set of other potential explanatory measures were available from the WERS to use as controls. These consisted of information from the manager's questionnaire about the workplace (listed in Chapter 2, Table 3). Logistic regression for dichotomous choice (0/1) variables and ordinary least squares regression for interval data were used to examine the determinants of the various performance measures.

Results of the WERS analyses on performance

The best defined models were those of sales value and labour turnover. The model of absence was the least well defined, possibly because the data are conceptually confused, as we suggested earlier.

Family-friendly policies in the private sector

After controlling for a wide range of structural and other HR practices, family-friendly policies were associated with small amounts of improved performance in the private sector.

Above-average **financial performance** was associated with:
• paternity leave
• job share.

Above-average **labour productivity** performance was associated with:
• parental leave (non-statutory)
• paternity leave
• the ability to change from full- to part-time hours
• having a higher number of family-friendly policies.

Improvements in **quality performance** were associated with:
• term-time only work
• the ability to change from full- to part-time hours
• offering help with childcare
• having a higher number of family-friendly policies.

Rising **sales value** was associated with:
• job share
• the ability to change from full- to part-time hours
• having a higher number of family-friendly policies.

Reduced **labour turnover** was associated with:
• job share
• flexi-time
• help with childcare
• working at or from home.

Absence did not have any benefits from family-friendly policies being present.

However, some performance measures appeared to suffer from the presence of certain family-friendly policies:
• flexi-time was associated with a reduction in financial performance;
• emergency leave was associated with increases in labour turnover;
• term-time work and possibly flexi-time were associated with increases in absence.

Having a family-friendly ethos was associated significantly with above-average financial, labour productivity, quality and sales performances.

The sizes of a selection of these effects are set out in Figures 6 and 7. On a base set of characteristics, the additional effects of having one (Figure 6) of the family-friendly policies or a number of them (Figure 7) are displayed. The models for labour turnover and absence were estimated on the whole sample, as well as on the private-sector samples only, since it was felt that these performance measures applied to all sectors, private and public. Some differences in the results are worth noting.

A reduction in labour turnover was associated with job share, flexi-time, help with childcare and working from or at home across both private and public sectors. However, in all cases there were interactions with other HR variables that reduced the significance of these associations when HR variables were entered. The bad effects of term-time employment on absence were not apparent in the sample covering both sectors, although the bad effects of flexi-time were repeated in both sectors.

Family-friendly effects and the good employer

We needed to consider whether the effects of family-friendly policies on performance noted above were specific to these policies or a feature of some companies being good employers. Separating out these possible scenarios is difficult, although an attempt was made to do this in order to address this issue[1].

---

[1] The good employer variable was derived from a factor analysis in which a large number of mainly HR practices recorded in the manager's questionnaire were entered. The resulting factors identified one factor with an eigenvalue greater than 1. The factor score for this factor was used in this analysis. The variables included were whether the following were used: teams; briefing; consultative committee; quality circles; employee surveys; a range of other forms of workforce consultation; manager's attitude towards trades unions; time to learn the job in main occupation; whether firm recruited female returners; extent of use of temporary workers; discretion needed in main job; has HR specialist on site or at head office; has family-friendly ethos; uses other fringe benefits; has equal opportunities policies; consults on equal opportunities; Investors in People award; performance-related pay; recent bad industrial relations; extent of use of regular overtime; pay above average last year; has profit-related pay.

Figure 6: Predicted probabilities of above-average performance, given contribution of family-friendly policy

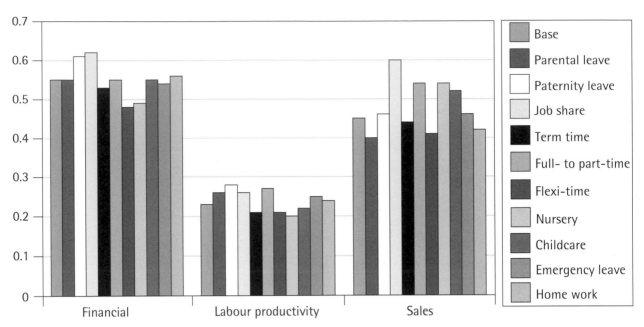

Note to Figure 6 and 7:
The base characteristics for Figures 6 and 7 are as follows: an establishment of 100-199 employees in an organisation of 2,000-9,999 employees; in manufacturing; a union; a multinational; trading in international markets; with labour costs of 50%-75% of total costs; few competitors; a share of non-managerial staff of 75%; female employees 40%; time to learn the job one to six months; equal opportunities medium; and an HR specialist at the establishment.

Figure 7: Predicted probabilities of above-average performance, by number of family-friendly policies

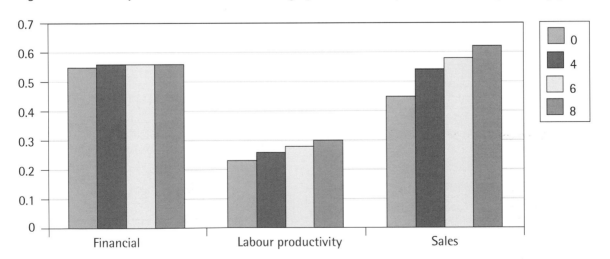

Figure 8: Predicted probabilities of above-average performance, by size of establishment (number of employees)

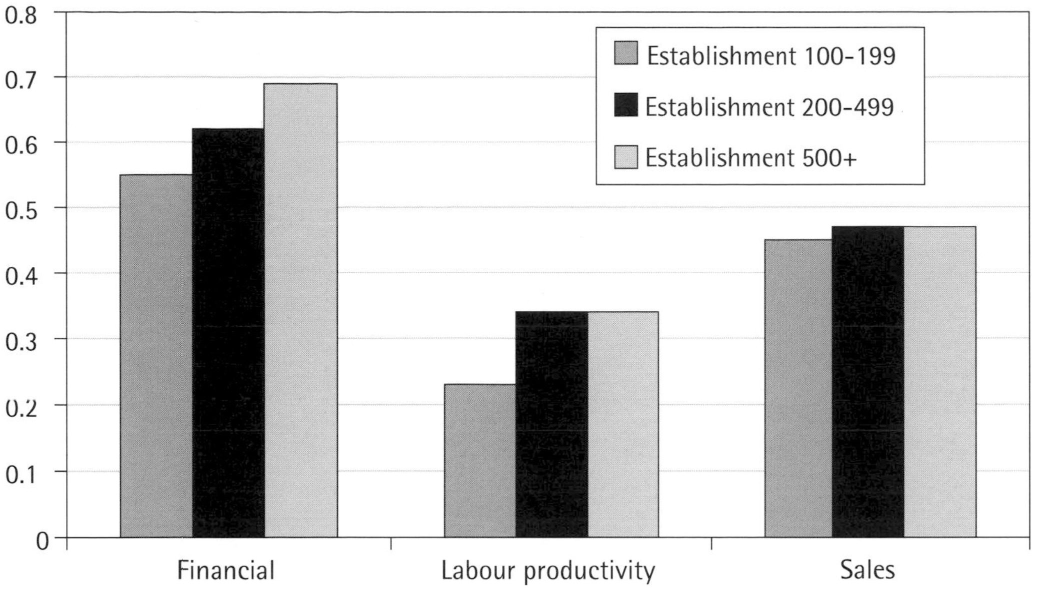

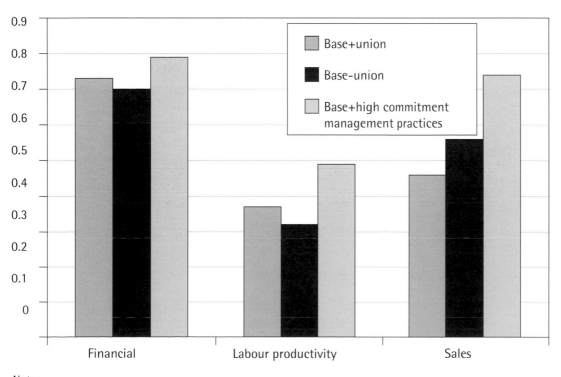

Note for Figures 8 and 9:
The base characteristics for Figures 8 and 9 are as follows: an establishment of 500+ employees in an organisation of between 2,000 and 9,999 employees; in manufacturing; a multinational; trading in international markets; with labour costs of 50%–75% of total costs; few competitors; a share of non-managerial staff of 75%; female employees 40%; time to learn the job one to six months; equal opportunities medium; and an IIR specialist at the establishment. Having a recognised union has been added to this set. Alternatively, a set of other characteristics were added: high commitment management; worker involvement in decision making; other fringe benefits; performance-related pay; and a family-friendly ethos.

Figure 9: Predicted probabilities of above-average performance, by union/high commitment management contributions

Note:
The base characteristic have a recognised union included (+), or removed (-), or a high commitment management practices added, but no union and predicted probabilities of above-average performance is recalculated each time.

There were clear (bivariate) correlations between the measure of being a good employer and the individual family-friendly policies in all cases except emergency leave. These results indicated initial support for the idea that good employers were also those offering family-friendly policies in British establishments. However, the correlations are far from being perfect at well below one half. Further analysis showed that the 'good employer' variable contributed a large amount of explanation to the variation in the performance measures. Whereas the family-friendly policy contributions were substantially less, family-friendly policies added to the explanation of performance over and above controlling for being a good employer.

Other controlling variables

A range of factors under each of these headings were found to be significant determinants of each type of performance. Most of these results were reasonable and intuitively plausible, although not wholly in accord with our expectations. While support was gained, from some performance measures, for the hypotheses about the effects of size, knowledge workers and HR practices the picture was shown to be complicated, partly by considering a range of performance measures alongside each other. A selection of effects on performance of size (Figure 8) and having a union or high commitment management policies (Figure 9) are displayed.

Conclusions

The British discussion about how far there is a 'business case' for employers to introduce family-friendly policies has been waiting for larger-scale survey data to complement the case study material that has accumulated. Representative data are important in order to test whether any potential benefits from family-friendly policies are restricted to certain organisations where conditions are favourable.

Our analysis, in the cross-section, of whether various components of private-sector business performance were affected by employers offering family-friendly policies to their employees has suggested that some benefits do exist after controlling for a wide range of other

determinants. In particular, the WERS data found associations between a family-friendly ethos in the establishment and most aspects of the performance of private-sector establishments. Also, small but significant associations were noted between particular performance measures and some of the range of family-friendly working arrangements for five of the six performance measures available. Since we are dealing with cross-sectional data, we cannot be sure that the family-friendly policies have caused the improvements in performance, but only that they are significantly correlated. In all cases, the effects noted were over and above those attributable to good employers having a bundle of policies, family-friendly policies being just one of the raft.

Absence did not appear to benefit from family-friendly policies being available. However, there is a need to take into account the fact that the statistics on absence were conceptually confused and probably the least satisfactory of the WERS performance measures. Drawing robust conclusions about the FTSE100 companies will have to await a longer run of performance data becoming available.

Conclusions

6

This research started out with a number of important questions about the nature and patterns of so-called family-friendly employment policies in Britain at the end of the 20th century. We have been able to go some way towards answering these questions through the analysis of the WERS data source. However, the position is likely to be fast changing, particularly as there are currently government and other initiatives to promote and encourage organisations to adopt more flexible working arrangements.

One important result from our analysis is that the answers to most of the questions addressed varies somewhat depending on the type of working arrangement under consideration. In this concluding chapter, we make some more sweeping generalisations, but we should not forget that the detail is important.

Employers and employees with family-friendly policies

The two sources of information from employers and employees on family-friendly working arrangements largely told the same story. Family-friendly policies were more common where there were:

- larger organisations and establishments
- public sector organisations and establishments
- lower degrees of competition
- recognised unions
- resources of HR and good performance
- high commitment management practices
- more involvement of employees in decision making
- stronger equal opportunities policies

- larger proportions of women in the workforce
- a highly educated workforce using discretion.

Human resource policies associated with being a good employer were likely to be associated with having family-friendly policies. In addition, unions were associated with having family-friendly policies. This finding contrasts with the view that the decline of unions was necessary for flexible working arrangements to come in. In fact, it seems that unions in both the public and private sectors have been instrumental in developing family-friendly solutions to the work–family challenges. Thus, the view that securing Britain's economic prospects needs to be tied to a non-unionised, minimally regulated, low waged economy is also challenged. More flexible family-friendly working arrangements have clearly developed in the context of both unionised workplaces and those that have adopted high commitment management strategies, rather than being either/or developments.

The findings also suggested that small- and medium-sized enterprises (SMEs) may be relatively family-unfriendly. However, against this there is evidence from case studies (for example Dex and Scheibl, 2001, 2002) suggesting that SMEs can have quite a lot of flexibility, although not the sort that necessarily gets counted in survey questions. This relation of size to family-friendly provisions remains, therefore, to be confirmed. Other studies have suggested that the lack of ability to substitute between different staff can act as a constraint on the provision of flexibility, more often at the higher skilled end (for example Dex and Scheibl, 2002). Our findings suggest that these constraints must have been overcome in many circumstances, given the larger amount of flexible working arrangements this group appeared to have access to.

Flexi-time, home working and emergency leave stood out from the list of other arrangements considered in a number of ways. Factors that were associated with employers offering flexi-time and emergency leave tended to be more related to their having a lower skilled workforce and to certain types of job – in the case of flexi-time, clerical and secretarial work. Home working was associated with a higher skilled male workforce but also was less likely where the needs of customers or the operations required more constant presence in the workplace.

Expected outcomes for employers from family-friendly policies

This research examined the potential effects of family-friendly working arrangements on employee commitment, the 'business case' and other measures of financial and HR performance. The most robust and striking outcomes were as follows.

- There were positive effects on employee commitment in private-sector companies from having family-friendly policies.
- Approximately nine out of every 10 establishments with some experience of these policies found them cost effective.
- Increases in performance were associated with having one or other family-friendly policy in the case of five out of six performance indicators.

A lot of emphasis has been placed on the 'business case' for having flexible working arrangements. On the basis of organisations that have adopted these practices, these results offer some support for the business case for flexibility, but the effects are small. Is this bad news? Well, for those hoping for greater effects, the results might be disappointing. On the other hand, the lack of sizeable negative effects from offering employees more flexibility has notable policy implications. If it helps employees, and they like it, as other evidence suggests is the case, the absence of bad effects on performance is a good reason for pressing ahead. The public sector is the one area in which some caution needs to be exercised.

Clearly, these findings challenge the idea that better performance results from cracking down on wages, increasing work intensity and increasing hours of work – the so-called low road to business success. In contrast, our findings are more in tune with the idea that an economy based on knowledge work and high amounts of value added, where workers have discretion and flexibility, is our best chance for success.

Implications for policy

If the desire is to encourage more British employers to adopt flexible working arrangements, then a number of implications follow from this research.

There are pockets of the economy where flexible working arrangements have made relatively few inroads. These are the pockets that need most attention: manufacturing industries; the non-union sector, where high commitment management policies are rare; male-dominated establishments. However, it is not a choice between unionised or high commitment management. Family-friendly policies can develop in both environments.

There are no guarantees that if other companies adopted the same practices they would reap the same benefits, since organisations that do not currently have flexible working arrangements may conceivably be a selected sample of those that would benefit least if they were to introduce them. However, the results certainly suggest that it is worth companies not currently offering such arrangements giving serious consideration to introducing them. Other research has found that some SME employers who resisted using flexible working arrangements did so because of traditional attitudes, and stereotyped and mistaken views. They also resisted changes in new technology (Dex and Scheibl, 2002). It would be a pity if employers missed potential performance benefits for these sorts of reasons.

Family-friendly working arrangements are more common among employers adopting HR policies and practices associated with the notion of being a 'good employer'. Good employers were also found to be associated with better performance outcomes. That good employers are more likely than others to have these sorts of policies is an argument that can be used as a lever in the process of encouraging the wider use of flexible arrangements.

From the perspective of employees who are eligible, the challenge for policy is to include men and men's workplaces within the remit. In some cases this involves tackling the introduction of flexible working in male manufacturing skilled craft-based workplaces. One other important element of the need to include more men with access and take up of family-friendly provision is the desire to equalise the cost to employers of such policies. If it is only employers of women who offer flexibility or leave to care for sick children, then any burdens of absence or disruption will fall unequally on employers of female parents, with employers of male parents having a free ride. In the long run, this will not be sustainable and may cause a reversion to greater discrimination in hiring practices.

Further research

Further research needs to be conducted in the following areas:

1. The extent of flexible working arrangements in SMEs.
2. The nature of employee commitment in the public sector.
3. The need to disentangle the role of traditional views versus genuine job constraints as potential barriers to more employers adopting flexible working arrangements.
4. The performance effects on businesses from having family-friendly working arrangements, when objective measures linked to individual enterprises become available for a large and preferably longitudinal sample.

References

Airy, C., Hales, J., Hamilton, R., Korovessis, C., McKernana, A. and Purdon, S. (1999) *The Workplace Employee Relations Survey (WERS) 1997-98 technical report*, London: NCSR.

AON Consulting (2000) *UK @ work 2000: Workforce commitment in the new millennium*, London: AON Consulting.

Bailyn, L., Rayman, P., Harvey, M., Krim, R., Read, R., Carre, F., Dickert, J., Joshi, P. and Martinez, A. (1998) *The Radcliffe–Fleet Project: Creating work and life integration solutions*, Cambridge, MA: Radcliffe Public Policy Institute.

Barringer, M.W. and Milkovich, G.T. (1998) 'A theoretical exploration of the adoption and design of flexible benefit plans: a case of HR innovation', *Academy of Management Review*, vol 23, no 2, pp 305-24.

Becker, H.S. (1964) 'Personal change in adult life', reprinted in R.G. Burgess (1995) *Howard Becker on education*, Buckingham: Open University Press.

Berry-Lound, D. (1990) *Work and the family: Carer-friendly employment practices*, London: IPM National Committees for Equal Opportunities and Pay and Employment Conditions.

Bevan, S., Kettley, P. and Patch, A. (1997) *Who cares?*, IES Report 330, Brighton: Institute for Employment Studies.

Bevan, S., Dench, S., Tamkin, P. and Cummings, J. (1999) *Family-friendly employment: The business case*, Research Report RR136, London: DfEE.

Bond, S., Hyman, J., Summers, J. and Wise, S. (2002) *Family-friendly policies and organisational decision-making*, York: York Publishing Services for the Joseph Rowntree Foundation.

Brannen, J., Meszaros, G., Moss, P. and Poland, G. (1994) *Employment and family life: A review of research in the UK (1980-1994)*, Research Series 41, Sheffield: Employment Department.

Bryson, C., Budd, T., Lewis, J. and Elam, G. (1999) *Women's attitudes to combining paid work and family life*, London: The Women's Unit.

Callender, C., Millward, N., Lissenburgh, S. and Forth, J. (1997) *Maternity rights and benefits in Britain*, London: PSI.

Casey, B., Metcalf, N. and Millward, N. (1997) *Employers' use of flexible labour*, London: PSI.

CIPD (Chartered Institute of Personnel and Development) (2000) *Labour turnover*, London: CIPD.

Coopey, J. and Hartley, J. (1991) 'Reconsidering the case for organisational commitment', *Human Resource Management Journal*, vol 1, no 3, pp 18-32.

Cully, M., Woodland, S., O'Reilly, A. and Dix, G. (1999) *Britain at work: As depicted by the 1998 Workplace Employee Relations Survey*, London: Routledge.

Daly, K.J. (1996) *Families and time: Keeping pace in a hurried culture*, London: Sage Publications.

Dex, S. (ed) (1999) *Families and the labour market*, London: Family Policy Studies Centre for the Joseph Rowntree Foundation.

Dex, S. and Scheibl, F. (1999) 'Business performance and family friendly policies', *Journal of General Management*, vol 24, no 4, pp 22-37.

Dex, S. and Scheibl, F. (2001) 'Flexible and family-friendly working arrangements in UK-based SMEs', *British Journal of Industrial Relations*, vol 39, no 3, pp 411-32.

Dex, S. and Scheibl, F. (2002) *SMEs and flexible working arrangements*, Bristol/York: The Policy Press/Joseph Rowntree Foundation.

Dex, S. and Smith, C. (2001a) 'Which British employees have access to family-friendly policies? An analysis of the 1998 Workplace Employee Relations Survey', Judge Institute Research Paper WP 17/2001, Cambridge: University of Cambridge.

Dex, S. and Smith, C. (2001b) 'Employees' access to family-friendly policies and practices', Judge Institute Research Paper WP16/2001, Cambridge: University of Cambridge.

Dex, S. and Smith, C. (2001c) 'Employee commitment as an outcome of family-friendly policies?', Judge Institute Research Paper WP 20/2001, Cambridge: University of Cambridge.

Dex, S., Smith, C. and Winter, S. (2001) 'Effects of family-friendly policies on business performance', Judge Institute Research Paper WP 22/2001, Cambridge: University of Cambridge.

Dex, S., Smith, C. and McCulloch, A. (2002) 'Employees' awareness of employers' flexible working arrangements', Judge Institute Research Paper, WP02/2002, Cambridge: University of Cambridge.

Dex, S., Scheibl, F., Smith, C. and Coussey, M. (2000) *New working patterns*, London: Centre for Tomorrows Company.

DfEE (Department for Education and Employment) (1998) *Meeting the childcare challenge*, Cm 3959, London: DfEE.

DfEE (2000) *Changing patterns in a changing world*, London: DfEE.

DoH (Department of Health) (1999) *Caring about carers: A national strategy for carers*, London: The Stationery Office.

DTI (Department of Trade and Industry) (1998) *Fairness at work*, Cm 3968, London: DTI.

DTI (2000a) *Work and parents: Competitiveness and choice*, Green Paper, Cm 5005, London: DTI.

DTI (2000b) *Work and parents: Competitiveness and choice, a research review*, London: DTI.

Evans, J. (2001) *Firms' contribution to the reconciliation between work and family life*, Paris: OECD Labour Market and Social Policy Occasional Papers.

Felstead, A., Jewson, N., Phizacklea, A. and Walters, S. (2001b) 'A statistical portrait of working at home in the UK: evidence from the Labour Force Survey', Unpublished paper, ESRC Future of Work Programme.

Felstead, A., Newson, N., Phizacklea, A. and Walters, S. (2001a) 'Blurring the home/work boundary: profiling employers who allow working at home', Unpublished paper, ESRC Future of Work Programme.

Forth, J., Lissenburgh, S., Callender, C. and Millward, N. (1997) *Family friendly working arrangements in Britain*, Research Report 16, London: DfEE.

Gallie, D. and White, M. (1993) *Employee commitment and the skills revolution*, London: PSI Publishing.

Golembiewski, R.T. and Proehl, C.W. (1978) 'A survey of the empirical literature on flexible work hours: character and consequences of a major innovation', *Academy of Management Review*, vol 3, pp 842-53.

Golembiewski, R.T. and Proehl, C.W. (1980) 'Public sector applications of flexible workhours: a review of available experience', *Public Administration Review*, vol 40, pp 72-85.

Goodstein, J.D. (1994) 'Institutional pressures and strategic responsiveness: employer involvement in work–family issues', *Academy of Management Journal*, vol 37, no 2, pp 350-82.

Gottlieb, B., Kelloway, E.K. and Barham, E. (1998) *Flexible working arrangements: Managing the work–family balance*, Chichester: John Wiley & Sons.

Guest, D. (1992) 'Employee commitment and control', in J. Hartely and G.M. Stephenson, (eds) *Employment relations*, Oxford: Blackwell.

Guest, D. (1997) 'Human resource management and performance: a review and research agenda', *International Journal of Human Resource Management*, vol 8, no 3, pp 263-76.

Guest, D., Michie, J., Sheelan, M. and Conway, N. (2000a) *Employment relations, HRM and business performance*, London; IPD, now CIPD.

Guest, D., Michie, J., Sheehan, M. and Conway, N. (2000b) 'Getting inside the HRM–performance relationship', Working Paper 8, ESRC Future of Work Programme.

Healy, G. (1999) 'Structuring commitments in interrupted careers: career breaks, commitment and the life cycle in teaching', *Gender Work and Organisation*, vol 6, no 4, pp 185-201.

Hogarth, T., Hasluck, C., Pierre, G., Winterbotham, M. and Vivian, D. (2000) *Work–life balance 2000: Baseline study of work–life balance practices in Great Britain*, Warwick: Institute for Employment Research, Warwick University.

Home Office (1998) *Supporting families: A consultation document*, London: Home Office.

Huselid, M. (1995) 'The impact of human resource management practices on turnover, productivity, and corporate financial performance', *Academy of Management Journal*, vol 38, no 3, pp 635-72.

Ingram, P. and Simons, T. (1995) 'Institutional and resource dependence determinants of responsiveness to work–family issues', *Academy of Management Journal*, vol 38, no 5, pp 1466-82.

IPD (Institute of Personnel and Development) (2000) *Employee absence*, IPD Survey Report no 13, London: IPD, now CIPD.

IRS (Industrial Relations Services) (2000) 'Who cares?', *IRS Employment Trends*, no 697, February, pp 2-16.

Lapdio, D., Reed, H. and Wilkinson, F. (1999) 'Changing midwifery: working conditions and the quality of care', Working Paper 136, ESRC Centre for Business Research, University of Cambridge.

Lewis, S. and Lewis, J. (1996) *The work–family challenge: Rethinking employment*, London: Sage Publications.

McRae, S. (1991) *Maternity rights in Britain: The PSI report on the experience of women and employers*, London: PSI.

Morrow, P.C. (1993) *The theory and measurement of work commitment*, Greenwich, CT: JAI Press.

Neuman, G.A., Edwards, J.E. and Raju, N. (1989) 'Organisational development interventions: a meta analysis of their effects on satisfaction and other attitudes', *Personnel Psychology*, vol 42, pp 461-89.

Osterman, P. (1995) 'Work/family programs and the employment relationship', *Administrative Science Quarterly*, vol 40, pp 681-700.

Perotin, V. and Robinson, A. (1999) 'Employee participation and equal opportunities practices: performance effects and potential complementarities', Paper given at *British Journal of Industrial Relations*/Workplace Employee Relations Survey 1998 Conference, London, September.

Purcell, K. (1997) 'The implications of employment flexibility for equal opportunities', Paper for British Universities Industrial Relations Association Annual Conference, University of Bath, 4-6 July.

Purcell, K., Hogarth, T. and Simm, C. (1999) *The costs and benefits of non-standard employment*, York: York Publishing Services for the Joseph Rowntree Foundation.

Rathbone Neilson Cubbold (1999) *Family-friendly employment survey 1998: The ethical view*, Bristol: Rathbone Neilson Cubbold Ltd.

Richardson, R. and Thompson, M. (1999) *The impact of people management practices on business performance: A literature review*, London: IPD, now CIPD.

Scholaris, D., Ramsay, H. and Harley, B. (1999) 'High noon on the high road: testing inside the black box of "high performance" work systems', Paper given at *British Journal of Industrial Relations*/Workplace Employee Relations Survey 1998 Conference, London, September.

Shepard, E.M., Clifton, T.J. and Kruse, D. (1996) 'Flexible work hours and productivity: some evidence from the pharmaceutical industry', *Industrial Relations*, vol 35, no 1, pp 123-39.

Spearritt, K. and Edgar, D. (1994) *The family-friendly front: A review of Australian and international work and family research*, Monash, Australia: National Key Centre in Industrial Relations, Monash University.

Thomson, K. (1995) 'Working mothers: choice or circumstance?', *British Social Attitude: The 12th report*, Dartmouth: Social and Community Research Planning.

Turner (1999) 'Strategic HR management, employee voice and organisational performance', Paper given at *British Journal of Industrial Relations*/Workplace Employee Relations Survey 1998 Conference, London, September.

Winter, S. (1999) *Family-friendly employment survey*, Bristol: Rathbone Neilson Cubbold.

Wood, S. (1999) 'Family-friendly management: testing the various perspectives', *National Institute Economic Review*, vol 172, no 2, pp 99-116.

Yeandle, S., Wigfield, A., Crompton, R. and Dennett, J. (2002: forthcoming) *Employers, communities and family-friendly employment policies*, Bristol/York: The Policy Press/Joseph Rowntree Foundation.

Appendix: The FTSE100 data (Financial Times Stock Exchange companies)

In order to satisfy the need for information by ethical investors, the stockbroking firm Rathbone Investment Management (Bristol) contacted FTSE100 companies to ask them to complete a structured questionnaire about their policies. When completed, a telephone follow-up was carried out to clarify data or to request further information. Dr Sally Winter collected these data. Survey questions that asked about family-friendly policies were included in 1996 and in a follow-up survey of the same companies in 1998. Of the 104 companies represented at the two dates, data were successfully collected in 1998 from 51 companies. A summary of the initial findings were published in Rathbone Neilson and Cubbold (1999) from a report by Winter (1999).

Rathbone Investment Management kindly gave us permission to use the existing data in an anonymised form to carry out further multivariate analysis. We have also attempted to make the data more complete. Telephone interviews were carried out with the 53 non-responders to the 1998 study to find out about their policies in 1998. In some cases it was not possible to obtain this information, for a variety of reasons. However, in 30 cases reasonably reliable information has been obtained from this exercise. To these survey data we have linked a set of company-specific performance measures obtained from their annual accounts, as deposited in DATASTREAM. In total, we had information from 81 of the 1998 FTSE100 companies on which to carry out analysis.

An analysis of these data was carried out which attempted to explain the performance measures using a limited set of explanatory variables (industry, turnover, labour intensity and family-friendly policies). Ideally, we wanted performance measures that post-dated the policy

information collected in the telephone interviews in order to determine the extent to which policies current in 1998 influenced the future performance of these large companies. However, we found that we were unable to construct even three-year averages from the database information for a sufficient number of companies to keep up a small sample size. Our results are, therefore, more like cross-sectional comparisons.

FTSE100 results

A breakdown of the means of the performance measures available revealed that operating profit per capita and changes in added value increased significantly as the extent of family-friendliness of FTSE100 companies increased at the cross-section as shown in Table 5 (Chapter 3). Other measures did not show any relationship with the extent of being family-friendly for this group of companies.

In the multivariate analysis, relatively few of the available explanatory variables were found to be significantly correlated with any of the financial performance measures, although this varied by performance measure. The model explaining the change in added value had the best fit. Operating profit had the second best model fit. The detailed results are in Dex et al (2001).

By comparison with the other determinants of business performance, the contribution of family-friendly working arrangements was relatively weak and often insignificant. In the case of percentage changes in value added and per capita operating profit, there was some evidence that pointed to family-friendly policies being associated with good performance. However, the evidence on whether family-friendly policies

Table A: Means of performance measures as related to extent of overall assessment of family-friendly policies of FTSE100 companies in 1998

Level of family-friendliness (1998)	Operating profit per capita (£) (1999)		% change in value added (1998-99)	
	(£)	(%)		
Low	20.7	(20)	17.9	(20)
Medium	33.8	(32)	18.6	(32)
High	76.4	(23)	27.2	(23)
Total sample N		75		75

Note:
Low/medium/high was an assessment made by the interviewer based on the number of policies the companies were offering but also their implementation and follow through.

affect the financial or productivity performance of FTSE100 companies was not strong. The FTSE100 data are interesting and important for their influence in the British economy, but are nonetheless small in numbers of cases.

The main limitation of this analysis was that the performance measures available did not capture the post-policy longer-term performance of these companies. It is perhaps not surprising that many of the models were not well specified. Further investigation would be required, when future years of performance data are available, in order to obtain more robust conclusions.